T0319003

Cambridge Elements ≡

Elements in Public and Nonprofit Administration
edited by
Andrew Whitford
University of Georgia
Robert Christensen
Brigham Young University

GENDER IMBALANCE IN PUBLIC SECTOR LEADERSHIP

Leisha DeHart-Davis
University of North Carolina at Chapel Hill

Deneen Hatmaker
University of Connecticut

Kimberly L. Nelson
University of North Carolina at Chapel Hill

Sanjay K. Pandey
George Washington University

Sheela Pandey
Penn State Harrisburg

Amy E. Smith
University of Massachusetts Boston

CAMBRIDGE
UNIVERSITY PRESS

CAMBRIDGE
UNIVERSITY PRESS

University Printing House, Cambridge CB2 8BS, United Kingdom

One Liberty Plaza, 20th Floor, New York, NY 10006, USA

477 Williamstown Road, Port Melbourne, VIC 3207, Australia

314–321, 3rd Floor, Plot 3, Splendor Forum, Jasola District Centre,
New Delhi – 110025, India

79 Anson Road, #06–04/06, Singapore 079906

Cambridge University Press is part of the University of Cambridge.

It furthers the University's mission by disseminating knowledge in the pursuit of education, learning, and research at the highest international levels of excellence.

www.cambridge.org
Information on this title: www.cambridge.org/9781108708081
DOI: 10.1017/9781108761352

First published 2020

A catalogue record for this publication is available from the British Library.

ISBN 978-1-108-70808-1 Paperback
ISSN 2515–4303 (online)
ISSN 2515-429X (print)

Cambridge University Press has no responsibility for the persistence or accuracy of URLs for external or third-party internet websites referred to in this publication and does not guarantee that any content on such websites is, or will remain, accurate or appropriate.

Gender Imbalance in Public Sector Leadership

Elements in Public and Nonprofit Administration

DOI: 10.1017/9781108761352
First published online: June 2020

Leisha DeHart-Davis
University of North Carolina at Chapel Hill
Deneen Hatmaker
University of Connecticut
Kimberly L. Nelson
University of North Carolina at Chapel Hill
Sanjay K. Pandey
George Washington University
Sheela Pandey
Penn State Harrisburg
Amy E. Smith
University of Massachusetts Boston

Author for correspondence: Leisha DeHart-Davis, ldehart@sog.unc.edu

Abstract: Women remain underrepresented at the highest echelons of the public sector, despite comprising half of the public sector workforce in the United States. To study this imbalance, we focus on the local government setting, which employs more than 60 percent of the public sector workforce in the United States. We use a problem-driven approach to examine gender imbalance in local government management. We employ multiple methods, inductive and deductive research, and different theoretical frames for exploring why there are so few women leaders in local government management. A qualitative analysis of interviews with thirty female local government managers and assistant managers allowed us to discern patterns that shed light on gendered workplace experiences, as well as barriers to pursuing the top job. A sequence analysis of the resumes of forty-one North Carolina county managers enabled us to detect gender differences in career paths that possibly preclude a higher percentage of women in top positions. Finally, we analyze secondary data collected on local government managers of 100 counties and 332 cities in North Carolina using the glass cliff theory as our explanatory framework. Our results suggest the women in local government management face a complex puzzle of gendered career experiences and circumstances that lend insights into gender-imbalanced leadership in this domain. We conclude with recommendations for future research and managerial action.

Keywords: gender, gender and leadership, gender-imbalanced leadership

ISBNs: 9781108708081 (PB), 9781108761352 (OC)
ISSNs:: 2515-4303 (online), 2515-429X (print)

Contents

1 Introduction

On January 12, 2016, Marcy Onieal – the manager of the Town of Waynesville, North Carolina – closed the monthly council meeting by requesting a point of privilege. She began by saying, "I have no additional reports tonight, but if I may take a brief moment, I would simply like to address the elephant in the room, since I have apparently become that elephant."

Onieal had been hired in 2012 as a change agent for the town. The previous manager had served for 20 years, during which time the town had no performance evaluation system and the paychecks of 150 employees were individually signed by the former manager. Onieal had accomplished the job she was hired to do, including implementing employee performance evaluation, restructuring the public works department, and creating a nepotism policy.

But in December 2015, the *Smoky Mountain News* ran the headline, "Still Trapped by the Delicate Dance of a New Town Manager, Waynesville's Marcy Onieal Faces a Double-Edged Sword Daily." The article reported employee complaints about Onieal's leadership style and how it differed in comparison with that of her predecessor: "For nearly two decades, the town had hummed along comfortably under the guiding hand of Lee Galloway. He was easygoing, affable, paternal – a boss people were happy to work for their entire careers." The article continued, "Onieal has a no-nonsense, brass-tacks, analytical style that some aren't used to, especially in a woman in a small Southern town. A workaholic by nature, Onieal is faster-paced, more formal, more business-like than employees were used to." Marcy Onieal was fired by the Board of Aldermen on January 15, 2016.

Onieal's experiences provide a perfect Rorschach test for a range of theories that seek to explain gender imbalance in organizational leadership. Her actions as a leader evoked role congruity theory, in which her behavior as a leader contradicted cultural norms for women as nurturing, accommodating, and acquiescent (Eagly and Karau, 2002; Eagly and Carli, 2003). The approbation of the former male manager's informal and paternal style is consistent with status theory, which posits that cultural beliefs assign competence and social significance to certain social groups – most notably men – rather than to their disproportionate grip on power and resources (Ridgeway, 2001: 27). As role congruity theory would predict, Onieal's behavior as a leader violates her status as a woman, triggering dislike and, ultimately, backlash (Correll and Ridgeway, 2003). The reference to the former manager as being paternal evokes Camilla Stivers' *Gender Images in Public Administration*, which contends that masculine imagery dominates public administration practice, challenging the ability of women to lead (Hutchinson, Walker, and McKenzie, 2014). And being hired after a long-term public manager and charged to make significant organizational changes represents a classic glass cliff scenario, in which women disproportionately land leadership positions that are professionally precarious (Ryan and Haslam, 2007).

While these theories provide snippets of insight about gender-imbalanced public sector leadership, they do not, either singly or taken together, explain the persistent gender imbalance in public sector leadership. After all, women receive a higher percentage of Master of Public Administration (MPA) degrees than do men,[1] and desirable traits for public managers have evolved into a balance of culturally feminine and masculine traits (Duehr and Bono, 2006). Yet women still lag far behind men in their representation at the top of public and private organizations. Because no single theory can fully address this pervasive problem, we adopt a problem-driven approach to understanding gender-imbalanced public sector leadership.

Problem-driven research was first articulated by business professors Gerald Davis and Christopher Marquis in 2005 in an article in *Organization Science*. Davis and Marquis argued that organizational theory should move away from research that deductively tests a single theory; in their minds, doing so had produced little theoretical innovation in the field, and consequently, stale theories of resource dependency, new institutionalism, and population ecology were cited routinely without any evidence of their validity. This engagement and attachment to older theories produced variations – such as "reruns of old classics" featuring familiar plot twists and turns – that did little to provide a deeper understanding of important social problems. As an alternative, Davis and Marquis advocated for a problem-driven approach that would seek to explain the "whys" of real-world phenomena, with an emphasis on explanatory mechanisms. In the process, problem-driven research would eschew single theories in favor of a range of explanatory frameworks that uncovered the mechanisms of phenomena, namely, the "cogs and wheels behind the regression coefficient."

Gender-imbalanced public sector leadership is ripe for problem-driven research, albeit not a common topic for public administration scholars. More often than not, public administration scholars examine issues related to representative bureaucracy, gender dynamics in public organizations, and the effects of diversity management within organizations (DeHart-Davis et al., 2018). While these are important topics, the "whys" of gender-imbalanced public sector leadership remain elusive, even as women remain underrepresented as leaders of federal, state, and local government. Thus, our objective in writing

---

[1] www.naspaa.org/sites/default/files/docs/2018–12/2016–17-accr-data-report-final.pdf

this Element is to explore a range of potential explanations for gender-imbalanced leadership in the public sector to move us closer to a holistic explanation of why gender-imbalanced public sector leadership persists.

Having decided on a problem-driven approach to gender-imbalanced public sector leadership, our next tactic was to narrow the scope of our investigation to local government management. Local government management is, in many ways, an ideal laboratory for researching gender-imbalanced public sector leadership. It is the unit of government with which citizens have the most direct contact, whether paying utility bills, receiving healthcare, or reporting crimes in their neighborhood. Local government is also highly varied in functions making generalizability less of an issue (Nelson and Stenberg, 2017). Finally, the chief administrative officers[2] who run cities and counties remain overwhelmingly male,[3] despite the many affinity groups, leadership trainings, and opinion pieces seeking to diversify local government management.

We also chose to use multiple methods to investigate gender-imbalanced local government management. This choice enables us to examine gender imbalance from different angles and generate a more comprehensive picture of the problem. Accordingly, qualitative analysis of interviews with thirty female local government professionals allowed us to discern patterns of comments that shed light on the nature of local government management, as well as barriers to pursuing the top job. Analysis of the resumes of forty-one North Carolina county managers enabled us to detect gender differences in career paths that possibly preclude a higher percentage of women in top positions. Finally, we analyze secondary data collected on local government managers of 100 counties and 332 cities in North Carolina using the glass cliff theory as our explanatory framework. Glass cliff theory argues that women are more likely to land leadership positions in organizations with declining performance or circumstances that create higher professional risk. Using hierarchical binary logistic regression, we seek to explain the appointment of women as city and county managers as a function of measures of financial, political, and legal risk.

We report our findings in the following pages, which we begin by making the case that gender-balanced leadership is intrinsically valuable, beyond utilitarian arguments that focus on the benefits of women in leadership positions. Next comes a brief overview of the theoretical reasons why there are so few women in public service leadership positions. The following section is a history of the long and slow ascent of women in local government management positions. A discussion of the interview data follows, demonstrating the considerable

---

[2] We use the terms "chief administrative officers" and "city/county managers" interchangeably.
[3] https://icma.org/data-icma-women-members-profession

challenges faced by women who become local government managers. These themes will be familiar to scholars of gender in public administration but will also add fresh angles to existing theoretical narratives. Next, the sequence analysis of resumes reveals distinct career paths for women and men in reaching the managerial stage and suggests some ways that this may affect gender balance. Our exploration of secondary data follows, testing for the existence of a glass cliff in local government management and raising questions about the opportunities that exist in pursuing more or less risky positions. The final section is on implications of our findings for local government and public service.

2 The Need for Gender-Balanced Public Sector Leadership

After significant progress during the last century, the trajectory to gender balance has appreciably slowed. World Economic Forum's 2018 Gender Gap Report – tracking gender gap on the dimensions of economic participation and opportunity, educational attainment, health and survival, and political empowerment – notes, "Overall the gender gap has been reduced by 0.03% since last year and by 3.6% since 2006 . . . with current trends, the overall global gender gap can be closed in 108 years (p. 15)." Catalyst, a nonprofit focused on advocacy for women in the workplace, draws upon data on S&P 500 companies to show that the proportion of women dwindles as one moves up the hierarchy, with only 5 percent of chief executive officers (CEOs) being women. An Ernst and Young report (2017) notes that the percentage of women in public sector leadership positions globally hovers at about 30 percent. DeHart-Davis et al. (2018) provide similar statistics for US public sector leadership with women comprising 30 percent of senior executive service positions in the federal government (Riccucci, 2009) and 30 percent of US state agency heads (Bowling et al., 2006)

The need for gender balance in public sector leadership should not be a contested proposition. Indeed, we accept the need for gender balance in other domains. Most of us, for example, accept the desirability of gender balance in human population on an axiomatic basis, without a need for well-developed arguments and evidence. The gender-balance proposition in public leadership, however, faces a court of skeptics. In a recent review of public sector diversity research, DeHart-Davis et al. (2018) elaborate on two prominent lines of argument in the public administration literature aimed at the skeptics. The first of these lines of argument, the theoretical lens based on representative bureaucracy, has a long history in public administration literature. The second, the so-called business case for diversity management, draws upon a range of social psychological theories to argue that women bring unique skills and talents to leadership that make them a valuable asset to organizations (Herring, 2009).

Despite significant differences in theoretical terms and framing, there are remarkable lines of similarity between arguments based on representative bureaucracy and business case theories. Both sets of theories take an instrumental approach, theorizing that gender balance and gender representation lead to desirable social, public policy, or organizational outcomes. Although empirical research in different contexts provides support for these theories, there are notable instances of findings that run counter to theoretical expectations. Some of these inconsistencies can be overcome by better incorporating contextual factors. For example, organizational socialization can weaken the effects of active representation defined as the propensity of members of underrepresented groups to act on behalf of others from the group (Saidel and Losocco, 2005; Wilkins and Williams, 2009). Other inconsistencies may need careful consideration of underlying assumptions and theoretical framework. The concept of active representation based on a singular and binary conception of gender has been challenged by intersectionality theorists who argue that other aspects that confer marginal status (e.g., race and ethnicity, and sexual orientation) also need attention (see Breslin, Pandey, and Riccucci, 2017). Theories attempting to provide a business case for gender balance likewise run into problems. Business case theories for gender balance expressed in terms of valuable end goals – whether these goals are social, organizational, or public policy outcomes – have to contend with the mediating and moderating role of gender diversity because these effects may not be in alignment with valued outcomes (Breslin, Pandey, and Pandey, 2017).

How should we view the issue of gender balance in public sector leadership then? The ideal of gender balance in public sector leadership should have the same "taken-for-granted" sense as our expectations of gender balance in the human population. Thus, we should accept gender balance as a terminal value and view the lack of gender balance as a problem that needs vigorous engagement and attention. Such a perspective opens us up to the reality of the gendered nature of organizations and other institutions and invites us to consider how to reform and address the inequities perpetuated by the path-dependent nature of gendered organizations and institutions. Consider a simple example. In many western countries with high levels of gender equality, women continue to be underrepresented in science and technology. Many answers are offered for this state of affairs, among them the so-called "leaky pipeline." Contrast this with the state of affairs in former Eastern European countries. A recent edition of the Economist notes the following, "Eastern Europe bucks the global trend, according to a recent report from Leiden University in the Netherlands. In Lithuania, 57% of scientists and engineers are women. Bulgaria and Latvia follow close behind, at 52%." This balanced state of affairs is not a result of programs to plug the "leaky pipeline" or other liberal initiatives. Instead, it is the result of choices made decades ago under Soviet influence to require gender balance.

Gender balance in public leadership, thus, should be regarded as a terminal value and not instrumental as is the case in prominent theories. If we see gender balance as a terminal value, then addressing the accompanying organizational, social, and structural barriers to achieving it become imperative. Accordingly, we make the enabling assumption that gender-balanced public sector leadership is right regardless of the instrumental benefits that it brings, and we thus seek to uncover a range of factors driving gender imbalance in public leadership, focusing on the case of local government management.

3 Why Do So Few Women Lead?

Before delving into the history of women in local government leadership, let us briefly review the theories of why there are so few women in leadership positions. Three key theories – on social roles, social status, and stereotyping – give us complementary viewpoints on the challenges that women face in ascending the organizational ladder.

Social roles delineate expectations for people who occupy a position or social category (Eagly and Karau, 2002: 574). Historical divisions of labor drive gendered social roles, with women serving as homemakers and men as bread-winners (Eagly and Kite, 1987; Stivers, 2002). This divided labor has translated to beliefs that women do and should behave communally and men do and should behave agentically. Communal attributes include being helpful, nurturing, gentle (Johnson et al., 2008), friendly, unselfish, concerned with others, and emotionally expressive (Eagly and Johnson, 1990). Agentic behaviors incorporate independence, mastery, assertiveness, and competence (Eagly et al., 1992); dominance (Williams and Tiedens, 2015), strength, masculinity, and tyranny (Johnson et al., 2008); control, aggression, ambition, forcefulness, and self-sufficiency (Brems and Johnson, 1990). Because leadership is associated with agentic attributes, women who engage in the agentic behavior required of leaders violate gender role expectations (Eagly and Karau, 2002; Eagly and Carli, 2003). The act of merely assuming a leadership role incurs gender penalties, as male leaders tend to be more favorably evaluated than female leaders, an advantage that intensifies in male-dominated environments (Eagly, Makhijani, and Klonsky, 1992). Social role incongruity may be one reason that women are less likely to bend rules as they ascend the organizational ladder, because doing so involves the exercise of discretionary power that violates social roles (Portillo and DeHart-Davis, 2009).

Status theory argues that widely held cultural beliefs inhere competence and social significance to certain categories of people rather than to the disproportionate power or resources they hold. Gender comprises one type of social hierarchy, with men holding a higher status than women. While status beliefs are held at the cultural or societal level, individuals vary in alignment to their own beliefs (Ridgeway, 2001: 643). Like social role theory, status theory predicts a backlash against women who behave agentically. But status theory adds the violation of social hierarchy, with women asserting authority over others, to the reasons that female leaders elicit negative reactions and resistance (Ridgeway, 2001: 648). Under these circumstances, women are less likely to pursue top positions or they encounter much greater barriers after reaching those positions.

Gender stereotype theory also seeks to explain the dearth of women in leadership positions. As Madeline Heilman identified in 2001, stereotypes are beliefs about how groups of people do act (descriptive stereotypes) and should act (prescriptive stereotypes). Gender stereotypes encompass beliefs that women are (and should be) "kind, helpful, sympathetic, and concerned about others," while men are (and should be) "aggressive, forceful, independent, and decisive" (Heilman, 2001: 658). When women assume leadership positions, they violate both descriptive and prescriptive beliefs about feminine behavior and thus encounter disapproval that can culminate in negative evaluations, professional successes being marginalized, less cooperation and poorer attitudes from employees, and dislike and derogation (Heilman, 2001: 661–670).

These theories all seek to shed light on gender-imbalanced organizational leadership but employ slightly different explanatory lenses for doing so: the constrained societal roles that women are expected to fulfill, the lower social status ascribed to women, and categories of beliefs about how women do and should behave all challenge the ability of women to behave as leaders. As we progress through the Element, we will see all of these angles represented, beginning with the history of women in local government management.

4 Women in Local Government Management: A Historical Overview

A formal awareness of gender-imbalanced leadership in local government management dates back to 1973, during a time of both social turmoil and social progress. Congress had passed the Equal Employment Opportunity Act the year prior; President Nixon appointed the first female cabinet secretary; and Billy Jean King defeated Bobby Riggs in a Battle of the Sexes tennis match. The Vietnam War ended as the Cold War raged, the Watergate investigations kicked into gear, and oil and gas prices were astronomical. The nation was engaged in an internal struggle with its own traditions, norms, and deeply cherished beliefs.

During this time of social upheaval, the International City/County Management Association (ICMA) devoted a special issue in its magazine *Public Management* to the status of women in the profession (1973). The article, written by then-staffer Claire Rubin, calculated an abysmal 1 percent of ICMA membership comprising women, including only 15 of 2,523 US cities run by women, and only 24 elected women mayors.

ICMA followed up this special issue by forming the first Task Force on Women in the Profession in 1974, which issued its report in 1976. At the time, ICMA's membership of 2,802 chief administrative officers included only 36 women, roughly 1 percent. The task force report characterized obstacles faced by women as pre-entry barriers and post-entry barriers. The term "pre-entry barriers" described broader social forces, both formal and informal, that stood in the way of women obtaining managerial positions, for example, lack of educational opportunities and a lack of role models. The report also identified seven post-entry barriers, which affect women after they enter the local government workforce. Notable among these barriers were differential performance expectations, stereotypes, and role expectations. Women were expected to work "smarter and harder," and with less support from the organization. The task force documented a range of rampant stereotypes about women that had an invisible but profound effect on opportunities available to them in the management profession. In an insightful comment on gendered role expectations and the need to change them, the report noted, "it is necessary for women and men to consciously examine the stereotypes and myths surrounding working women to see if there is any validity, and not to generalize that all women fit certain assumptions" (p. 8).

In 1978, women still made up only about 10 percent of municipal managers at the department head level or above (Burns, 1980). By 1986, there were more than 100 female city managers (Slack, 1987), showing incremental progress, but still fewer than 10 percent. Ten years later, there were 432 women city managers in ICMA's database, making up 12.1 percent of total chief administrative officers (CAOs) (Fox and Schuhmann, 1999).

The second ICMA Task Force on Women in the Profession issued its report in 2014 under the leadership of Bonnie Svrcek, ICMA's second female president, and chaired by Pamela Antil and Tamara Letourneau (ICMA, 2014). With sixty-eight task force members at hand, the report highlighted inequities of senior level recruitment in the city management profession that effectively discriminated against women candidates. At the time of the 2014 report, 14.4 percent of ICMA's member CAOs were women, representing roughly 516 members. The 2014 report presented widespread perceptions of gender bias by elected leadership at the local level and strongly recommended expanding gender bias awareness and anti-harassment training to elected officials. Referring to the first task force report, the second task force acknowledged lowering pre-entry social barriers but underscored the persistence of age-old barriers, including the role of elected officials that tend to be mostly male in the selection of the local government manager, the protégé (or "good old boy") system, female stereotypes, and lack of upward mobility assignments for women (p. 33).

Women now make up only 17 percent of city or county managers,[4] and women of color comprise a miniscule 1.39 percent of managers (ICMA, 2012). While these percentages are abysmally small, they nonetheless represent gains for local government management, a profession that has been slow to incorporate women into its leadership ranks. We next venture into the patterns of interview results that reveal possible explanations for why local government management has been so slow to become gender inclusive.

5 Gendered Career Paths in Local Government Management

Currently, women make up almost half the labor force in the United States and have been earning more undergraduate and graduate degrees than men for quite some time (Catalyst, 2019). Even with these advances though, gender diversity in the upper levels of public sector organizations remains elusive (Riccucci, 2009). While existing research has examined the individual, organizational, and institutional factors associated with attaining leadership positions, less is known about the career paths that lead to these positions (Acker, 1990; Bowling, Kelleher, and Jones, 2006; Smith and Monaghan, 2013). We use sequence analysis methods to examine the career paths of forty-one women and men who have reached top-level positions in county governments in the US state of North Carolina. While some studies have examined career paths in public service (e.g., Watson and Hassett, 2004; Buckwalter and Parsons, 2000), to our knowledge, none of these studies have employed sequence analysis techniques. The purpose of our career path analysis is to identify types of career patterns in local government and the extent to which there are gender differences in careers in this sector.

---

[4] https://icma.org/data-icma-women-members-profession

Our findings suggest there are two types of careers that lead to the top-level county manager positions and that the careers of the women and the men who hold these positions differ based on gender. Next, we describe the data and methods used in our career path analysis, present our results, and offer concluding remarks.

5.1 Data and Methods

Our sample comprises complete career paths for forty-one individuals who held county manager positions in North Carolina county governments. To generate career histories, we used resumes provided by the county managers. To gather resumes, the research team sent email requests to all 100 county managers in the US state of North Carolina between fall 2018 and spring 2019. We followed our first email request with two follow-up email requests. In the end, we received 41 resumes (41 percent of county managers). In addition to resumes, we used LinkedIn profiles and internet searches to confirm information about the managers' careers as well as demographic characteristics.

While a sample size of forty-one career histories for county managers in North Carolina is small, this sample provides ample opportunity to investigate career patterns in public service for several reasons.[5] First, by restricting our sample to a particular type of local government manager in a single US state – county managers in North Carolina – we control for variation in careers that may occur because of geography or type of local government (i.e., county vs. city). Second, using geographic and local government type restrictions limits our sampling frame to only 100 individuals (all 100 county managers in North Carolina). While 41 resumes is a small number, it is more than 40 percent of the population of county managers in North Carolina. Finally, with its highly professionalized workforce and strong county government system, county managers in North Carolina can be considered an extreme case allowing for detailed examination of careers in local government, particularly with respect to gender imbalances in leadership (Patton, 1990).

Resumes were coded to establish a complete career path for each individual. For each year of employment through March 2019, the type of employment was coded from a set of ten categories. *Local government manager* included top-level positions such as city, county, or town manager. *Local government second-level manager* included positions such as assistant town manager or deputy town manager. *Local government other* included any other local government employment. For example, positions such as budget analyst or planner were

---

[5] We follow Blair-Loy's (1999) sample selection rationale in her examination of career patterns for fifty-six women in finance careers.

included in this category. *Public sector other* included any other nonlocal government public sector employment. For example, employment in state agencies or the federal government is included in this category. *Nonprofit* included employment at nonprofit organizations. *Primary/secondary education* included employment in positions such as school principal or teacher. *Higher education* included employment at institutions of higher education in positions in offices of human resources, budgeting, information technology, and others. *Private sector* employment included any positions in private sector organizations, often working in sales, consulting, human resources, and budgeting, among others. The *other* category encompassed all employment not included in the prior categories. In this category, we include service in the military, for example. Finally, we also coded for *gaps in employment*. We code employment years in this category when no employment was listed for certain years.

In addition to complete career histories, we also collected individual-level characteristics for each of the managers in our sample. We coded resumes for types of educational degrees, the number of local governments the manager has been employed in, the number of years in the workforce, the number of years working in public service, and whether or not the manager was promoted to their current manager position from within the organization. We coded the gender of each manager based on pronouns used in publicly available biographies and online news articles.

Our sample is comprised of 8 women (20 percent) and 33 men (80 percent). This distribution is similar to the gender distribution for the population of county managers at the time of data collection (also 20 percent women). In general, the managers in our sample have accumulated substantial human capital with advanced educational degrees and considerable years of work experience, particularly in public service. Of the individuals in our sample, 71 percent had a graduate degree and 46 percent had an MPA degree specifically. On average, the managers in our sample have been in the workforce for 26 years, in public service positions for 25 years, and in their current position for 5 years. Almost half our sample began their careers in local government (44 percent), with a third (32 percent) being promoted to their current county manager position from within the county. Managers in our sample have been employed in, on average, four different local governments and in two different top-level positions in local governments.

5.2 Sequence Analysis of Career Paths

We use sequence analysis methods with the career histories in our sample to generate a set of career patterns for county managers (Abott, 1995; Brzinsky-Fay,

Kohler, and Luniak, 2006). Sequence analysis first identifies how similar each career path is to all other career paths in the dataset and then arranges career paths into groups based on similarity. It uses a set of ordered events as the unit of analysis, making this an ideal method for analyzing career histories (Abbott, 1995; Blair-Loy, 1999; MacIndoe and Abbott, 2004; Joseph, Boh, Ang, and Slaughter, 2012; Smith, Hatmaker, and Subedi, 2015).

Our data comprise year-by-year career histories for each of the forty-one county managers in our sample. For each county manager, we have a career sequence that indicates the type of organization of employment for each year they are in the workforce. For example, a hypothetical career sequence of nine years might include three years in a nonprofit organization, then two years in higher education, and finally four years as a local government manager.

Our sequence analysis begins with optimal matching or alignment methods (MacIndoe and Abbott, 2004). Each possible pair of career paths is compared in order to generate a dissimilarity matrix. For our data of 41 career sequences, this results in 820 unique comparisons. The dissimilarity matrix is generated by counting the number of changes that would need to be made to each pair of sequences in order to make them align. Changes that swap one type of employment for another are called *substitutions* (e.g., trade employment in a local government for employment in a nonprofit) and those that insert or delete an element of a sequence are called *indels* (e.g., insert a year of employment at a state agency). Both types of changes, substitutions and indels, have costs associated with them.[6] The sum of the costs associated with the total number of changes is the measure of dissimilarity for each pair of sequences, with higher numbers indicating more dissimilarity between the two career paths.[7] The dissimilarity measures for each pair of sequences are then combined to generate a matrix displaying a measure of dissimilarity for each possible pair of career sequences.

In the final step of the sequence analysis, we employ Ward's clustering method to arrange the sequences into groups based on similarity (Ward Jr., 1963).[8] While Ward's clustering method reveals multiple solutions, each with

[6] We set indel costs to be 0.10 of substitution costs. Citing the work of Blair-Loy (1999) and Carpenter (1996), MacIndoe and Abbott (2004) suggest such cost setting in order to detect sequence groups that are substantively important.

[7] There are many possible combinations of substitutions and indels that will result in alignment between career sequences. The optimal matching process chooses the combination that minimizes the cost of alignment based on the Levenshtein distance (Levenshtein, 1966; Brzinsky-Fay et al., 2006).

[8] Ward's method is considered an agglomerative hierarchical clustering method, here, using the dissimilarity measures generated during the optimal matching process. Ward's clustering method works iteratively by first treating each individual sequence as its own cluster and then adding clusters together one at time until all clusters have been joined into a single cluster. Ward's takes

a different number of clusters, we choose the optimum number of clusters based on visual inspection of the dendrogram produced by the cluster analysis and theoretical considerations (Mooi and Sarstedt, 2011). We use Stata statistical software to perform the sequence analysis and rely on guidance from MacIndoe and Abbott (2004) and Brzinsky-Fay, Kohler, and Luniak (2006) for our specification and interpretations.

Finally, we generate descriptive statistics for individual managers and the career patterns identified by the sequence analysis. We use these descriptive statistics to describe and label the career patterns revealed in our analysis and to compare career paths by gender.

5.3 Findings of Sequence Analysis

Figure 1 is a dendrogram representing the career clusters identified by the sequence analysis. Beginning on the horizontal axis of the dendrogram, the vertical lines represent each of the forty-one county managers in our sample. From the dendrogram, we discern two distinct career patterns for the county managers in our sample. Applying the career types conceptualized by Hall (2004), we label the career patterns revealed in our analysis *traditional* and

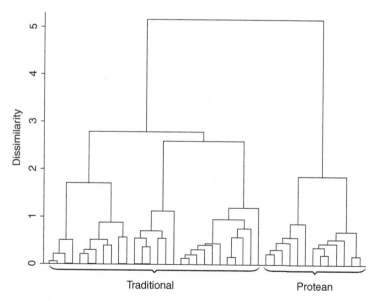

Figure 1 Dendrogram for cluster analysis of career patterns

---

an analysis of variance approach to minimize the sum of the squared deviations from the mean dissimilarity of the cluster (Ward Jr., 1963).

Table 1 Description of county managers by career pattern

	Traditional (n = 28)	Protean (n = 13)	Total (n = 41)
% women	21.4	15.4	19.5
% with graduate degree	75.0	61.5	70.7
% with MPA	57.1	23.1	46.3
% started career in local government	53.6	23.1	43.9
% promoted to top-level from within	25.0	46.2	31.7
% with private sector experience	39.3	46.2	41.5
% working only in local government	29.3	7.7	31.7
Avg years in workforce	28.1	22.5	26.3
Avg years in current position	6.6	2.4	5.2
Avg years in public service	27.1	21.5	25.3
Avg years to first top-level position	12.2	20.3	14.8
Avg # of local governments	5.0	2.9	4.3
Avg # of top-level positions	2.6	0.9	2.1

protean. These career patterns represent two pathways to leadership positions in local government. Tables 1 and 2 present descriptive statistics for each career pattern, and we discuss each career pattern next.

5.3.1 Traditional Careers

We label the first career pattern *traditional* because the career paths in this group reflect what we might consider to be a traditional career where individuals select a career field when they enter the workforce and continue employment in the field throughout their career (Hall, 1976, 2004). Traditional careers tend to be driven by the organization, where advancement is of central importance, commitment to the organization key, and interorganizational mobility is limited (Hall, 1976, 2004). For some, careers in public service in particular, take on the characteristics of traditional career paths (Smith, Hatmaker, and Subedi, 2015). In our data, traditional careers are dominated by experience and training specific to local government, though not always with the same organization. The traditional career pattern here includes work

Table 2 Percent of work years in sector by career pattern

	Traditional (n = 28, 786 work years)	Protean (n = 13, 292 work years)	Total (n = 41, 1078 work years)
Local government	79.5	77.1	78.9
Top-level manager	53.2	12.3	42.1
Second-level manager/ director	13.7	6.2	11.7
Other position	12.6	58.6	25.1
Other government	6.6	1.7	5.1
Nonprofit	0.5	0.3	0.5
Education	1.7	5.2	2.6
Primary/secondary	0.0	1.4	0.4
Higher education	1.7	3.8	2.2
Private sector	11.2	9.9	10.9
Other	0.5	2.4	1.0
Gap	0.3	3.4	1.1

in the same local government throughout a career as well as movement between local governments during a career.[9]

The majority of the managers in this group began their careers in local government (54 percent) with the remaining managers starting primarily in other nonmunicipal government organizations or the private sector (18 and 21 percent, respectively) and a few in either higher education or other types of organizations (7 percent). Of the aggregated work years in this group, 80 percent have been spent in local government, and almost 30 percent of the managers in this group have worked only in local government during their career. Managers in this group tend to have advanced degrees (75 percent) with 57 percent of the managers holding a master's degree in public administration (MPA), a degree specific to public service careers. Thus, managers in this group are developing human capital – experience and education – for careers in local government (Becker, 1993).

Additionally, the career patterns in this group also reflect an accumulation of social capital specific to local government (Brass, 1995). On average, managers in this group also have worked in five different local governments, held almost three top-level positions in these governments, and have held their current

---

[9] The traditional career pattern identified in our data displays elements of the static, horizontal, and vertical career patterns described by Buckwalter and Parsons (2000) and the ladder climbers, lateral movers, long servers, and single-city careerists described by Watson and Hassett (2003).

county manager position for almost seven years with only one quarter of the managers being promoted to their current position from within the county. Movement among positions within local governments and holding visible leadership positions may generate a cohesive network of social capital with tight ties among members concentrated in local government (Borgatti and Foster, 2003). Most of the managers in our sample (68 percent) and almost all of the women in our sample (75 percent) fall into this group.

5.3.2 Protean Careers

The second career pattern, we label *protean*. We label this group protean because, while their career paths have been dominated by work in local government, careers in this group reflect more variation in the types of organizations individuals worked at through their careers, where they started their career, and their academic training.[10] In contrast to traditional careers, protean careers are driven by the person, freedom and personal growth are central motivations, and personal satisfaction is the driving force (Hall, 1976, 2004). Unlike traditional careers, protean careers tend to be boundaryless often involving moving between different organizations (Arthur and Rousseau, 1996; Gubler, Arnold, and Coombs, 2014; Inkson, Gunz, Ganesh, and Roper, 2012).

Like those managers who fall into the traditional career pattern, those in the protean group, in the aggregate, have also spent a large proportion of their work years (77 percent) in local government. Though the types of positions held within local government differ across the two career patterns. In our data, work years in traditional careers were spent in top- and second-level positions in local government (53 percent of work years), while protean careers were spent in other positions in local government (59 percent of work years). However, the managers in the protean group tend to take more time than those in the traditional group to reach their first manager position (20.3 years and 12.2 years, respectively).

Protean careers, in contrast to traditional careers, include more time spent working in a variety of other sectors predominately the private sector (10 percent), education (5 percent), other types of organizations or an employment gap (6 percent). Less than a quarter (23 percent) started their careers in local government, while the remaining managers began their careers in the private sector (31 percent), education (23 percent), and either nonprofits, other types, or had an employment gap (23 percent). Only one of the managers in the protean group has worked exclusively in local government. In addition, while the

---

[10] The protean career pattern in our data, to some extent, reflects the mobility between sectors that characterizes the proactive career path defined by Buckwalter and Parsons (2000).

majority of the managers in the protean group also have an advanced degree (62 percent), only 23 percent have an MPA. This career group is smaller than the group of traditionalists containing only 32 percent of our sample, including only 2 of the 8 women in our sample.

5.3.3 Gendered Careers

In addition to the career patterns revealed in the sequence analysis, an analysis of careers by gender indicates several differences in the careers of the women and men who serve as county managers. Tables 3 and 4 describe the characteristics of these careers by gender. In general, the women managers in our sample had careers focused primarily on local government whereas the men in our sample had careers with more variation. Women tended to be narrow, yet deep, in their accumulation of both human and social capital, while men tended to be broader in their accruing of capital. Similar gender differences in careers have been found in other public sector career contexts (Smith, Hatmaker, and Subedi, 2015).

All but one of the women managers in our sample began their career in local government and all but two spent their entire careers in local government. Almost all (94%) of the aggregated 214 work years for the 8 women managers in our sample were spent in local government. The remaining work years were spent in only two sectors, higher education (4%) and other government organizations (2%). Women also tend to spend less of their time in local government in

Table 3 Description of county managers by gender

	Women (n = 8)	Men (n = 33)	Total (n = 41)
% with graduate degree	62.5	72.7	70.7
% with MPA	50.0	45.5	46.3
% started career in local government	87.5	33.3	43.9
% promoted to top-level from within	50.0	27.3	31.7
% with private sector experience	0.0	51.5	41.5
% working only in local government	75.0	24.2	34.0
Avg years in workforce	26.8	26.2	26.3
Avg years in current position	4.7	5.4	5.2
Avg years in public service	25.8	25.2	25.3
Avg years to first top-level position	16.9	14.2	14.8
Avg # of local governments	3.8	4.5	4.3
Avg # of top-level positions	1.6	2.2	2.1

Table 4 Percent of work years in sector by gender

	Women (n = 8, 214 work years)	Men (n = 33, 864 work years)	Total (n = 41, 1078 work years)
Local government	93.9	75.2	78.9
Top-level manager	36.9	43.4	42.1
Second-level manager/ director	21.5	9.3	11.7
Other position	35.5	22.5	25.1
Other government	1.9	5.9	5.1
Nonprofit	0.0	0.6	0.5
Education	4.2	2.2	2.6
Primary/secondary	0.0	0.5	0.4
Higher education	4.2	1.7	2.2
Private sector	0.0	13.5	10.9
Other	0.0	1.3	1.0
Gap	0.0	1.4	1.1

top-level positions (37% of work years for women, 43% of work years for men). Though, women also tend to spend more time in second-level positions (22% of work years for women, 9% of work years for men) and take more time to reach the top-level positions (17 years and 14 years, respectively). This may reflect what Eagly and Carly (2007) term the "labyrinth" – the path to leadership for women, as compared to men, is not clear and direct. Rather women must be aware of and persist through puzzles, which may or may not be explicit, throughout their careers. None of the women in our sample have worked in the private sector, other organizations, or nonprofit organizations. When compared to the men, a smaller proportion of the women have advanced educational degrees (63% of women, 73% of men). Yet, when compared to men, a larger proportion of women have MPA's specifically (50% of women, 45% of men).

In contrast, only about a third of the men in our sample (33%) began their careers in local government with the remaining men beginning their careers in the private sector (30%), other nonmunicipal government (15%), education (9%), nonprofits (3%), and other types of organizations or a gap in employment (9%). Less than a quarter (24%) have spent their entire career in local government. In the aggregate, men have spent a smaller proportion of their work years in local government (77%), yet more of this time in top-level positions (43%). The remaining work years for the men in our sample were spent in a variety of sectors with 14% in the private sector, 6% in other government organizations,

2% in education, and 3% in other organizations or with a gap in employment. More than half of the men (54%) also have private sector experience.

On average, the women and men in our sample have been in the workforce for about the same amount of time (27 and 26 years, respectively) and in public service for the same amount of time (26 and 25 years, respectively). However, on average, women have held fewer local government top-level positions (1.6 for women, 2.2 for men) and worked for fewer local governments (3.8 for women, 4.5 for men). Women, on average, have held their current manager position for less time than the men in our sample (4.7 years for women, 5.4 years for men), but also take longer to reach their first manager position (16.9 years for women, 14.2 years for men).

5.4 Summary and Implications of Sequence Analysis

Our analysis of career paths reveals two career patterns that lead to top-level leadership positions in county government as well as differences in the careers of the women and men that reach county manager positions. However, our analysis has several limitations. First, our sample of forty-one career histories is small. While this purposive sample allows us a detailed examination of career patterns, our findings are not generalizable to local government or public service more broadly. Though, our findings are in agreement with others who have studied careers in public service (Buckwalter and Parsons, 2000; Smith, Hatmaker, and Subedi, 2015; Watson and Hassett, 2004). Second, there are few women in our sample. However, the proportion of our sample that are women reflects the reality of the county manager profession. Future research could use different sampling strategies in the local government context or public service more broadly to increase both the sample size and the number of women in the sample. Finally, the sequence analysis is largely descriptive in nature allowing us to identify career patterns in our data, but not why these career patterns exist. Additional research, some of which is included in this Element, can help shed light on the career choices individuals make and how organizational and institutional factors shaped those decisions.

In our data, traditional careers are characterized by work experience and educational training focused on local government. Managers with tradi-tional careers are building narrow, yet deep, human and social capital specializing in local government. Most of the women in our sample have traditional-type career patterns. While our data do not reveal why women tend to have such patterns, this finding is similar to other studies of public service careers that find women who reach leadership positions tend to build careers primarily in the public sector while men exhibit careers marked by movement between the private and public sector (Smith, Hatmaker, and Subedi, 2015).

While also characterized by experience and training in local government, protean careers demonstrate more variability. Managers with protean careers are also building human and social capital, though not focused solely in local government. Careers in the protean pattern demonstrate more interorganizational mobility and training in a variety of disciplines. Only two of the women in our study fall into this career pattern category. While human and social capital influence career advancement (Metz and Tharenou, 2001) the different nature of capital generated by each career pattern may also influence career outcomes in different ways.

6 Gendered Experiences in Local Government Management

> *Well yeah, I mean I think implicit and explicit bias are real and they play into our daily interactions. ... those things are still very apparent. When I walk into the room I'm always going to be the, well maybe not for a long time but for now, I'm the youngest, I'm usually the only woman, or definitely the only black woman, and so those three things, they're apparent, and they influence people's initial assessment of my ability or my competency, what I'm bringing to the table. So those things are real, and I do think that it's important that I'm always prepared, and I am engaged in relationship building because that's one of the best ways to conquer some of those issues because we all have implicit and explicit bias.*

This quote from a city manager illuminates several barriers women face as local government manager. First, there is the sense of being an outsider – the "other" and the "only" in terms of multiple aspects of her identity – and how her difference influences others' perceptions of her ability. Then there's implicit and explicit bias that shapes day-to-day workplace interactions. Finally, there's the sense that she must engage in battle, arming herself with allies and constant, extensive preparation to "conquer" the issues. Taken together, these factors offer a glimpse of why there exists a disproportional number of women at the top of local government organizations.

This section seeks to provide further evidence to address the question of "why so few?" women serve as local government managers and assistant managers. We examine work experiences of thirty women who are local government managers using data collected through interviews. We focus especially on experiences that we believe contribute to the persistence of gender imbalance in local government management. In the next sections we discuss our methods for data collection and analysis. We then focus on how diversity and inclusion and work–life balance influence the decision to pursue, or not pursue, a local government management position. Next we examine the roles of mobility, mentors and networks in career advancement of local government management professionals. Finally, we explore the gender dynamics that accompany local government management jobs. We conclude with implications of our findings for gender-imbalanced local government management.

6.1 Research Methods

The research team included six faculty from five universities across the United States and five research assistants from those universities. Our interview questions focused on the interview participants' career experiences in local government. An advisory board of seven local government managers and assistant managers reviewed the interview protocol, suggested interview candidates, and made suggestions for improvements. This portion of our research was supported through a contract with the International City County Managers Association. Accordingly, ICMA staff also reviewed the interview protocol and made suggestions for additional questions.

We identified interview candidates using the advisory board and ICMA staff. The participants were recruited via email invitations from the principal investigator, who identified the project purpose and promised confidentiality. Once interview candidates agreed, individual researchers emailed a signed consent form outlining that the interview results would be held in confidence and that the report would not contain any identifying information.

The research team conducted thirty interviews with women who are currently working at the highest levels of local government. Fourteen interviews were conducted in-person and sixteen over the phone. The geographic distribution of interview participants breaks down to nineteen from the Southeastern United States, seven from the West Coast, six from the Midwest, four from the Northeast, and one from Canada.

Interviews were recorded by the research team and transcribed by a professional transcription service. To analyze the data, the research team first used MaxQDA, software for qualitative data analysis, to conduct an initial coding of the data. This initial coding identified data where specific keywords and phrases related to gender imbalance of women leaders and in organizations based on our literature review. Members of the team then manually coded transcripts using both the themes from the initial coding and an inductive coding approach by open coding the transcripts and then combining codes and themes into higher-level categories (Strauss and Corbin, 1998). This coding used an iterative approach of going back and forth between the data and relevant literature to inform and deepen the analysis. One team member first manually coded the transcripts using an inductive approach, allowing themes to emerge from the transcripts. This coding was grouped into broad categories. A second team member then analyzed the data for differentiation within these broad categories, using the literature as well as the MaxQDA coding to inform this step. This process allowed for both a comprehensive and in-depth analysis of the transcripts.

6.2 Results

This section begins with patterns of interview results that shed light on why women do or do not pursue positions in local government management, including community, organizational and professional diversity, and work–life balance. Next we report on themes around mobility, networks, and mentoring, key factors for career advancement and support. The women in our sample talked about the need to be mobile and the value of mentoring and networks, as well as finding themselves on the periphery of informal networks. Finally, our findings focus on how gender affects the career and work experiences of women in local government management.

6.2.1 Deciding to Pursue (or Not Pursue) the CAO Position

While each of our interview participants chose a career in local government, many were quite selective in their decisions to pursue, or not pursue, particular positions. While some of the factors emerging from our interviews transcend gender and race, our participants also identified reasons related to being a woman, and in some cases being a woman of color, for their selectivity in pursuing a local government position. In particular, signs of diversity and inclusion and work–life balance emerged as factors that influenced some women in deciding whether or not to pursue a management job.

6.2.1.1 Community, Organizational and Professional Diversity

Conventional wisdom and empirical research suggest that people want to see others like them in the communities, organizations, and professions that they join. Relational demography is one theoretical link between the desire to see like others at work, home, and professionally (Tsui and O'Reilly, 1989; Wesolowski and Mossholder, 1997), particularly in the relationship between organizational diversity and job applicants who are not white male (Avery, 2003; Thomas and Wise 1999). Thus, one possible explanation for gender imbalance in local government management is that women are less likely to pursue positions in communities and organizations, or even leadership positions in the local government management profession, that lack diversity. Our interview findings bear out this contention.

For one deputy manager, community diversity was a nonnegotiable condition for applying for a position. She explains that, "Before I apply to a community, I look at the demographics. If there's 3% African American, I'm not going there. Somebody called me up about a city in California and the pay was amazing, right? But it was on an island and I looked it up demographically and it was like .45 percent something African Americans. Me and my husband would be the only people of color. No way would I do that. I'm not doing that to myself. But I'm very strategic about where I will and will not work." For this manager, the risk of being socially isolated based on race is not one that she was willing to take, not for her or her family.

One city manager identified diversity in elected and organizational leadership, as well as the inclusiveness of their actions and policies, as important factors when considering where to work. She explains, "I'm looking for organizations ... where there's diversity. Where there have been women in leadership positions so that I know there's a path that's already been cut there. ... I'm no longer interested in being the pioneer, being the first woman someplace. [One city], I interviewed there because the previous manager was a female. The mayor is a very strong female. There are two other females on the council. They're all very strong women. I mean they all support women's issues. I'm looking for an organization that is clearly pro-female. I'm looking for an organization that has the same values that I do. So they value education. They value a no-tolerance policy for harassment. They have some flexibility for people who have families." From this CAO's perspective, it wasn't just having women in place, but also having strong women in place, in an organization where policies send signals of gender inclusion (Feeney and Stritch, 2019).

Beyond the local government organization and community, the relative lack of diversity in local government management may (historically at least) have dissuaded women from applying for top management jobs; in other words, birds of a feather flock together (McPherson, Smith-Lovin, and Cook, 2001). Additionally, when there are few women in leadership, women have a hard time picturing themselves in such positions, resulting in the image of a local government manager not being a "possible self" (Hazel and Nurius, 1986). As one example, some of our interview participants felt that the historical lack of diversity within the leadership of the International City County Management Association had done just that. But a recent influx of more diverse leadership, through two people of color who had recently been appointed executive director and association president, some managers saw that the association and, by extension the profession, changing for the better. One manager explains the shift: "A lot of folks who would normally not register and come to ICMA because they didn't feel supported and would have liked to see more of themselves reflected and they've chosen not to attend, they actually came this last year. So, I'm hoping we continue to see that grow and I think that will be beneficial."

6.2.1.2 Work–Life Balance

The breadth and depth of local government responsibilities make these leadership positions demanding jobs. Several participants identified long work hours and limited balance between work and life outside of work as undesirable aspects of local government management positions that may deter women from pursuing top positions. A city manager relays her current state of fatigue: "Because right now, today, I'm exhausted. I'm in the thick of my life and nothing seems more appealing than just being able to wake up in the morning, drink my coffee, and have nothing to do."

The regular intensity of the local government management workload is compounded for women, who on average have greater caregiving responsibilities (Lee and Tang, 2015). For many organizations, ensuring that employees are not marginalized for their caretaking duties takes not just a structural shift, but a cultural one. As one participant noted in describing accommodations by the organization so she could care for an ill parent, "They're so used to cut and dry, and not realizing the demands that a woman has, or a caretaker has. And so, they're trying to loosen up and think outside of the box."

Several participants describe the time demands of a local government management position as incompatible with family responsibilities and relationships. One city manager spoke to this issue and, to some extent, lent credence to arguments that women "still cannot have it all" (Slaughter, 2012): "That is very challenging in this position, when you know, I've got like thirteen evening meetings a month. My kids are grown and gone and I'm an empty nester now, but to do that when you're, to be in a management position, it requires so many off-hour meetings, and to be a parent, I just can't drop everything and go get a kid that's puking at school. So, that I think, is the biggest, biggest hurdle. You have to have a very strong support system at home and a husband that can be flexible, because if you don't, and I certainly don't know how a single parent could do this job."

This last quote shows that it has been largely up to women – without much organizational support – to overcome workload barriers to local government management positions. The lack of organizational support likely deters some women from pursuing local government management positions. In support of this argument, caregiving responsibilities influenced the career choices made by some of the CAOs we interviewed: the city manager who made the "hard decisions" to "turn down jobs" because "being mom was my number one responsibility"; the city manager who was sought balance in jobs so that she could "be there for my family and . . . serve the community that I'm in" and the assistant city manager who avoided pursuing a manager position after her kids were grown and thought to herself, "I should have done this a long time ago, I really should have."

This last quote raises an issue of debate within local government management (and the work world in general). One side argues that work and family can indeed be balanced at the top management levels, which are accompanied by the flexibility and autonomy to control one's schedule. The other side makes the claim that, in 2020, female leaders should not be put in this position where they have to choose between family and career progression and the answer lies in changing societal norms and institutional structures that hinder both (Stivers, 2002). The merits of these arguments are less important for present purposes than the beliefs held by women who would otherwise be ideal candidates for local government management positions.

6.3 Career Advancement: Mobility, Mentors, and Networks

Career advancement is another gendered aspect of local government management, in particular with regard to geographic mobility, mentors and sponsors, and professional networks. For the managers we spoke with, geographic mobility enabled rapid ascent into CAO positions, mentors, and sponsors were key in attaining positions and developing professionally, and the professional networks developed over time advanced and sustained careers.

Regarding geographic mobility, one deputy county manager explained, "If you want to be a manager, you must be willing to relocate geographically." This argument is backed up with research suggesting that job turnover in the city management profession is common.[11] For women willing to relocate, this turnover can provide opportunities, but family support for relocation can be a requirement for doing so. Channeling Sheryl Sandburg via *Lean In*, one city manager considers her marriage a partnership: "My husband and I have been married for thirty-three years and he's been a partner. He has been willing to

---

[11] See David N. Ammons and Matthew J. Bosse, "Tenure of City Managers: Examining the Dual Meaning of 'Average Turnover,'" *State and Local Government Review* 37, no. 1 (2005): 61–71; Barbara C. McCabe, Richard D. Feiock, James C. Clingermayer, and Christopher Stream, "Turnover among City Managers: The Role of Political and Economic Change," *Public Administration Review* 68, no. 2 (February 2008): 380–386; Tari Renner and Victor S. DeSantis, "City Manager Turnover: The Impact of Formal Authority and Electoral Change," *State and Local Government Review* 26, no. 2 (Spring 1994): 104–111.

move when I've gotten opportunities, so we've moved all over the place . . .. He has had some professional sacrifices that he's had to make to allow me to grow my career." However, relocation may be less likely in dual-career families especially when there is inadequate employment potential for the working spouse.[12]

Interview participants also cited mentors as vital for career development. In most cases, managers we spoke with had a collection of local government management professions who opened professional doors, provided insights on common local government situations, and advocated for their advancement. One deputy county manager explained her strategy: "I sort of have a collection of people in experiences that serve in that role for me, and for me, the way it's played out, there's no one regular or constant. I don't have like a this is my mentor and we meet monthly for lunch, that sort of thing. I have people I can call on for certain situations for advice, for counter advice, you know, that we all know." This finding is consistent with the literature on mentors, in which professionals develop a relationship "constellation" or a developmental network (Higgins and Kram, 2001; Kram, 1985).

Networks also influence career trajectories of women in local government management. For almost all of our participants, the connections they have with other professionals made a difference in their career trajectory. Their experiences echo research that notes the importance of establishing relationships with key others in organizations for career progression (Podolny and Baron, 1997). For many participants, primary places to develop a network are conferences. As the participants noted, conference attendance is crucial because connections can give you access to jobs. As one deputy county manager illustrates in her advice to early career professionals, "Here's what you need to remember. You need to come to this conference because these are the people who can make phone calls for you and get you hired fairly quickly."

While networks are critical for developing professionally in local government management, they can be gendered. Some managers talked about being left out of critical networking opportunities over the course of their careers, such as outings with commissioners that included other male senior organizational leaders but excluded them. This pattern is consistent with the 2014 ICMA Task Force Report suggesting that 31 percent of women had been excluded from important networking opportunities based on gender. For example, one newly promoted city manager noticed that the invitations from the local university stopped coming. She explains that, " . . . all of a sudden the chancellor was

---

[12] Christine M. Reed and B. J. Reed, "The Impact of Dual-Career Marriage on Occupational Mobility in the Local Government Management Profession," *The American Review of Public Administration* 23, no. 2 (June 1993): 141–154.

inviting my planning director and my development director to dinner parties or Christmas parties. So, I had to tell a high-ranking female I knew at the university, 'Look it's not that I'm dying to go to these things. But, from a protocol standpoint, my staff shouldn't get invited to things at the president's house that I don't get invited to.'"

Golf emerged as one type of event that excluded women from important networking opportunities. An assistant county manager wryly observes, "I don't golf, so we joke that we're going to take up golf because then you can play hooky from the conference and its viewed as legit. So, I'm like, when is hiking going to be the thing that is okay for us to miss the afternoon sessions because we're going on a hike." Another city manager explains, " . . . Local governments are sort of a place where there's lots of camaraderie and so the guys went and they all played golf. Well, you know, they're not going to invite me to play golf with them, right?" These sentiments are consistent with research suggesting that women and people of color have less powerful networks that limit career opportunities (Collinson and Hearn, 1996; Kanter, 1977; McGuire, 2002).

6.4 Gender Dynamics in Local Government Management

Only a handful of interview participants felt that gender had *not* affected their local government management experiences. To illustrate, one manager suspected that her lack of gendered experiences was due to having a prior female manager who "paved the way" for her. A third manager had only one negative experience she attributed to sexism, explaining that, "I've really had very few experiences that I felt in any way were a challenge or held me back in any respect." The following excerpt illustrates one such comment:

> I'm one of those, and I guess I've been fortunate in that I haven't really run up against any of the stereotypes and discrimination that a lot of women do, or maybe, I just don't take it as discrimination. You know, I look at it as I've got a job to do whether I'm female or whether I'm male, and I just do my job. And yes, there's not a lot of us around. There's far more than there used to be, and sometimes, I'm like, "Good grief. Will they just give it a break," you know? . . . Sometimes, we discriminate against ourselves, because we're women, or because we're black, or because we're Hispanic, or because we're Asian. But, the sooner all of us accept that we're managers, and we all have the same job to do, I think we're going to be a whole lot better off.

While this manager acknowledges the existence of discrimination against women – as well as the possibility that she is not picking up on that discrimination – she does not perceive her own experience as having been influenced by her gender. Furthermore, she believes that a manager's identity can help overcome the challenges that women and people of color face in the profession. However, importantly, for the remaining research participants, gender and race (for women of color) permeate the experience of being a local government manager. As the city manager quotes at the beginning of this section explained: "Implicit and explicit bias are real and they play into our daily interactions. So, whether I'm in a rural area or a large urban city, those things are still very apparent."

6.4.1 Visibility and Invisibility

Being a woman or person of color in local government means sometimes being "the only one" in the room. Recognizing that her only status might create tough challenges, one manager's family worried about her choice of a local government management career, saying "You're in this job. I don't hear anybody doing what you're trying to do. You're very much in this white man's world. Are you going to be okay?" Other managers talked of sometimes feeling "isolated" and "uncomfortable" in advance of meetings knowing they would be the only in the room. One deputy county manager describes this feeling:

> And you know, honestly, there would be times when I would know that, okay, I've got this meeting that so and so's going to be in here. I know that's going to be uncomfortable, and so . . . I mean, you just have to prepare yourself. I had this guy who used to tell me things like, "Well, think about it this way, when there's something you really are not comfortable with, fifty years from now it won't make a damn bit of difference, and you can get through it." So, I just would have to use some . . . little tips and tricks to kind of get through. But, you know, I would show up, I'd say what needed to be said, and we'd move forward.

Some women were not only the only woman in the room, but they were also the first woman or woman of color in their community to reach this level. As one town manager shared, "They'd never had a female, of course. Certainly had never had any African American folks." These pioneers discussed how the organization sometimes did not quite know "what to do with them" as well as the level of skepticism or surprise with which they were met.

Several participants described how their communities were slow to adapt to or embrace women leaders and others described the resistance to women as leaders. Some managers recounted being told that their communities were "not ready" for a female in a managerial role, that some men "don't like reporting to women," or that department heads were afraid of "being told what to do by a woman."

Being "the only" or "the first" put women in a position where their identity as a woman or woman of color was often spotlighted or highlighted (Foldy, 2012;

Hatmaker, 2013), particularly in ways that questioned whether or not they really belonged or were qualified for their position. As a result, the managers often expended energy trying to convince their doubters. They discussed needing to prove themselves, often over and over, as explained by one participant, " . . . it was very, very time consuming in trying to get them to understand that women can do this. I always felt like I was trying to prove something all the time." The need to demonstrate competency is echoed in the quote below by another manager. Noting her status as the only woman in the room, the manager feels compelled to prove not only that she is competent, but also that she is exceptional at her work.

> *Again, I think being in that nontraditional role, most of the time I was the only woman in the room. I was the only African American woman in the room many times. But I believe that it's really important to be competent and to be exceptionally good at what you do, and I think if you are then you rise to the top, like cream. You know, you rise to the top. I always set very high standards for myself. I would do my own research, I would take work home, I would work harder because I was kind of in a different environment.*

In both these narratives, the managers felt the need to be more prepared and to work harder in order to demonstrate their competency – a common strategy for women in male-dominated professions (Hatmaker, 2013). Women and their work are often subject to heightened scrutiny, particularly in male-dominated work contexts (Kanter, 1977). Perhaps this is why women are less likely to bend rules as they ascend the organizational ladder (Portillo and DeHart-Davis, 2009); the additional scrutiny of being at the top leads to a greater reluctance to exercise discretionary power. In another example, one manager of color referred being under "a different kind of microscope" than the typical white male manager. Another manager explains that not only did she ensure she was prepared, she actively took measures to ensure that she was better in anticipation of comparisons to male counterparts; although directly unspoken here, the underlying impression is the assumption that she would be found lacking in these comparisons.

> *I would say not so much with race as more so in gender that there are things that I had to make certain that any work or project that I worked on that I double-checked, I triple-checked, that I was at least 10 times better to make certain that when I spoke that I knew exactly what it was that I was talking about or chose maybe not to speak on the subject if I wasn't well versed, because I knew that at any given point and any given time more than likely I would be up against or compared to a male counterpoint and more often than not it was a white male counterpart.*

The language used in informal settings can make women feel invisible, particularly in meetings attended mostly by men. Below an assistant county manager and a town administrator describe being rendered invisible in meetings:

> . . . *it's like being in a locker room, but I try really hard not to let them see that some of the conversation I find insulting. Because once you do that you're dead because they'll sort of smell blood in the water and it will be their sport. But I have my counterpoint, the other assistant manager has been constant through all of this too and he's been a strong support. So, just two months ago I was in a meeting and actually an interim manager for the other woman who was out on maternity leave started a conversation by saying, "Gentlemen," and I tapped my counterpart and I said, "I'll meet you guys back at the office, okay. I'm not needed here."*
>
> . . . *at a meeting where I convened a bunch of men to talk about a big problem we're having related to the organization and running waste water and got up and the other senior man, I won't say who it is, got up and said, "Thank you gentlemen." And I thought really? Are you serious? Really?*

In both of these cases, the managers cite instances where the language used in meetings ignored their presence. Research on gender-exclusive language indicates that it is ostracizing for women. In one experiment, research subjects who were exposed to gender-exclusive language in a job interview were less likely to want the job (Stout and Dasgupta, 2011). For the local government management profession, gender-exclusive language is yet another discouraging cue that women do not fit the mold of the traditional local government manager.

6.4.2 Gendered Expectations, Bias, and Stereotypes

Managers also spoke about the effects of stereotypes gendered role expectations on their professional experiences. For example, it was not unusual to hear from participants that they had been mistaken for subordinates or service professionals at some point in their careers. Managers reported being asked to take notes or make coffee. As one manager explained, "I think my race and my gender have affected me maybe not the way some people answer the question. I think often the level of professionalism, the level of skill, the level of ability that I bring to every situation, I think it surprises people . . .."

Women also encountered assumptions that they were the sole caregiver for their children. One CAO recalls being asked, "'Who's taking care of the kids?' because, they couldn't conceive that my husband could be at home, right?" In an overt form of gender discrimination, one assistant manager was ruled out as a candidate for CAO "because she's a mom with kids." Sometimes these gendered expectations were communicated as early as the recruitment process, as one manager recounted below.

> *As much as people say they don't discriminate against women sadly there is discrimination out there, so when you are interviewing, I interviewed, at one point, for a community when I was pregnant and I had a male elected official ask me how are you going to balance this new child with the responsibilities of this community? And I thought to myself, "Are you going to ask a new father that question?" The recruiter was in the room and said you do not need to answer that, but at the same time, even if he didn't ask it, he's thinking it, right? So that's unfortunate and I think those types of factors, as much as progresses we have made as a nation, those factors still come into place and I think hurt women in their advancement.*

Gendered expectations about who makes a good leader also overshadowed the professional interactions for many of our participants. Some managers experienced the "think manager-think male" bias, which associates men with traits such as autonomy, assertiveness and control that are typically thought of what makes an effective leader (Schein, 1975). Sometimes this bias manifested itself as doubt expressed by colleagues, community members, or others from outside the organization, as explained below by one manager of color.

> *Other times they don't believe you are the city manager and I've lived through disaster recovery issues, where my assistant city manager is a white male, about 6'3" and all the outside authorities would go to him thinking he was the city manager, and he would point to me. And I knew how to respond ... people don't always identify you as being the person in charge or being the leader in the room.*

The hurdles arising from others' view of women's appropriateness for top management jobs were sometimes even higher when a woman replaced a male manager. For women of color who step into a role previously held by a white male manager, this bias was felt along both gender and racial lines, as explained in an example from one manager of color.

> *I also think there are expectations of you when you're female and again, some of them are overt and some of them are not. I followed a really wonderful, very traditional and male, white male leader here. And he had a very particular way of doing things and because I did things differently, I think lots of times, my first year here people would say, "Well you're just not the leader he was." And it's like, no, I'm different. And I think that was really, even though people didn't intend it, I think that was sort of latent sexism. Like there is an accepted way of doing things and it's the way the white guy did them.*

Gendered expectations, biases and stereotypes fit right in with theories suggesting that women encounter challenges as leaders because their behavior violates (1) beliefs about how women do and should behave (Heilman, 2001), (2) narrow social roles ascribed to women (Eagly and Karau, 2002) and beliefs that assign less social status to women (Ridgeway, 2001).

6.5 Discussion of Interview Results

Taken as a whole, our findings point toward experiences that send signals – both subtle and blatant – that women in local government management are an anomalous exception to the white male rule. While a handful of managers did not see their gender or race affecting their experiences, most spoke about the ways that it did. Our findings echo those of a great deal of prior research. For example, similar experiences have been reported in research on women in male-dominated professions, including engineering, medicine, finance, law enforcement, firefighting, and pilots (e.g. see Cassell, 1998; Germain, Herzog, and Hamilton, 2012; Hatmaker, 2013; Hulett, Bendick, Thomas, and Moccio, 2008; Roth, 2006). The women in our study experienced the stereotypes, gender bias, and gendered role expectations that continue to be embedded in patterns of interaction, organizational structures and cultural expectations that benefit men and disadvantage women (Ibarra, Ely, and Kolb, 2013: 64).

Women in management face a double bind because of the mismatch between the masculine qualities that are believed to make a good leader and stereotypically feminine characteristics (Eagly and Carli, 2007; Ibarra, Ely, and Kolb, 2013: 65). Women are assumed to be less able leaders because of gender stereotypes that ascribe qualities such as compassion, caretaking, and collaboration (Eagly and Carli, 2007; Ibarra, Ely, and Kolb, 2013; Sanchez-Hucles and Davis, 2010). And masculine traits such as decisiveness, assertiveness, and independence are associated with good leaders but when women exhibit these traits they are considered to be less likeable, arrogant, or abrasive (Eagly and Carli, 2007; Ibarra, Ely, and Kolb, 2013: 65). This gender bias serves to inhibit women's progress to the top echelons of organizations, and then questions their presence once they are there. To complicate matters further, barriers to advancement are not the same for white women and women of color, and women of color in leadership roles face more complex situations because of the intersectionality of their gender and race (Bell and Nkomo, 2001; Breslin, Pandey, and Riccucci, 2017; Rosette, Koval, Ma and Livingston, 2016; Sanchez-Hucles and Davis, 2010). The experiences of women of color are shaped by both sexism and racism, by both gender and racial stereotyping (Bell and Nkomo, 2001; Rosette, Koval, Ma and Livingston, 2016; Sanchez-Hucles and Davis, 2010).

Women who are local government managers, especially women of color, face what Roberts and colleagues (2018) call a "double-edged sword of visibility and invisibility" – on the one hand they stand out, yet at the same time they are rendered invisible through language and actions from others, often those in the majority group (Roberts, Ely, Mayo and Thomas, 2018). Managers in our study were sometimes the only women or women of color in the room, which, as we saw in our findings, can be isolating and spur extra effort to prove themselves worthy of a seat at the table. Racial dynamics also surfaced, as some managers experienced subtle and blatant signals calling attention to their "not white" status.

There are two sides of the coin to visibility. It can be positive, drawing attention to women and women of color who are the only one in the room and giving them the chance to show off their skills and perform (Roberts et al., 2018). Yet benefits do not always manifest themselves, especially when they and/or their difference is spotlighted such that they feel the need to constantly prove themselves and work harder than others or take effort to redirect the attention or interaction (Foldy, 2012; Roberts et al., 2018). This extra effort expends energy that men, particularly white men, often do not need to expend, and it can be exhausting and time-consuming (Hatmaker, 2013; Roberts et al., 2018). And women and women of color may find themselves less visible in places that can be key to career advancement – such as in informal networks – and more visible in ways that are not advantageous. As demonstrated by our interview findings, these moments of visibility and invisibility often leave indelible impressions and influence career choices.

When women local government managers experience interactions in which gendered role expectations manifest themselves, their status and authority as a leader can be undermined. As we saw, some managers were mistaken for subordinates or service professionals and were asked to undertake subservient tasks – making coffee or taking notes. Expectations that women should be the caretaker at home also emerged in the interviews. These interactions signaled to participants that they are viewed as a woman, or as a mother or wife, first, while their professional identity as a local government leader takes a backseat (Hatmaker, 2013). And as a result, they again feel the need to prove themselves time and time again. Many of our participants related how they "worked hard to take gender out of the equation-to simply be recognized for their skills and talents" (Ibarra, Ely, and Kolb, 2013). That is, they redirected interactions and engaged in impression management to be viewed as a professional first, with the high status conferred with that identity, rather than as a woman, wife or mother (see also Hatmaker, 2013). Without this added effort, these interactions and gendered role expectations serve to hold women back.

Although many of our participants spoke of being "the only" or "the first," the women of color in our sample nearly always fell into these categories, rendering them to a "double outsider" status (Catalyst, 2004; see also Bell and Nkomo, 2001). Our participants, especially the women of color, spoke of interactions that at times sidelined or derailed them and undermined their authority. These interactions questioned their very presence in leadership roles and led to a sense of heightened scrutiny. Similar to the African-American managers in Bell and Nkomo's (2001) study, they spoke of being held to different standards than their colleagues or their predecessors. Our findings overall are not necessarily unique; for example, a Catalyst (2004) report found similar experiences among corporate African-American women leaders. But our study indicates that, fifteen years after the Catalyst report and in a sector that generally espouses a commitment to diversity and inclusion, similar patterns of marginalization persist. Existing efforts to dismantle barriers may not be sufficient or they may not be working as intended. As Roberts and colleagues note, "When African-American women are underrepresented in an organization's senior leadership roles despite robust academic credentials and work experience, their struggles often suggest a broader problem: a workplace that fails to offer *every* employee equal access to opportunities for growth" (Roberts et al., 2018: 131, original authors' emphasis).

Roberts and colleagues (2018: 131) also speak to the resilience and perseverance women of color needed to overcome these experiences and barriers. But they emphasize the importance of institutional support –relationships with managers, mentors and sponsors who recognize their abilities, provide feedback, create opportunities, give them a safe space to take risks, and commit to their support (Roberts et al., 2018: 131). However, without the right context these relationships will not develop. It's up to local government organizations to create the setting where these relationships can develop and thrive. Organizations must also equip mentors, managers, and sponsors with a clear understanding of the obstacles women, and especially women of color, face and how to dismantle these barriers and enable women to overcome those that remain.

In fact, many of our participants emphasized the importance of mentors and networks for their career development and advancement, and for both instrumental and psychosocial support. Yet they also related experiences where they were ascribed outsider status and remained on the periphery of important interactions and informal networks. Research has long established the importance of mentors and networks to career development – networks of mentors and of more informal relationships can provide access to an array of key resources and connections (Higgins and Kram, 2001; Kram, 198;

Burt, 1992; Podolny and Baron, 1997). But the differential networks of women and men in organizations, where women do not enjoy comparable access to support, informational, and power networks in organizations, can lead to different career results (Burt, 1992; Ibarra, 1992, 1997; Ibarra, Ely, and Kolb, 2013; Podolny and Baron, 1997). For women of color, this differential and outsider status can be even more pronounced (Bell and Nkomo, 2001; Combs, 2003). While professional organizations such as ICMA can offer networking opportunities to influential colleagues outside a woman's home organization, this does not absolve local government organizations from doing more to solve this issue. In addition to equipping managers with the understanding of the unique challenges women and women of color face, organizations may also consider evaluating and rewarding managers for their mentorship and sponsorship activities (Hatmaker and Park, 2013).

Many issues of work–life balance disproportionately affect women and, as such, are crucial to address for a profession seeking to diversify its leadership ranks. Many of our participants talked about the stresses and strains of navigating the boundaries of work and family (Smith and Hatmaker, 2017). For some their responsibilities outside of work influenced their career path in terms of the positions they considered or accepted. Others discussed the inevitable spillover of local government management responsibilities beyond the typical work day and the sometimes all-consuming nature of the work. Such demands – long hours, 24 × 7 availability, and the sacrifice of self for total devotion to work – create an environment where women struggle to reconcile the competing spheres of work and home (Correll, Kelly, O'Connor, and Williams, 2014). In fact, the conflict between women's care obligations and many professions' long work hours is one explanation of why women's careers may stall and why gains in equality at work have stagnated (Padavic, Ely, and Reid, 2019). The experiences described by our participants were emblematic of the gendered division of labor, where men are expected to be the breadwinners and women are expected to be the caregivers (Davies and Frink, 2014) manifested itself in their workplace interactions. Such interactions serve to sideline and marginalize women, placing their identity as mothers or wives in the forefront. They are viewed as caretakers first, managers second, and these gendered expectations serve to maintain the gender inequality at the top levels of local government. As a result, women's workplace dedication may be questioned more frequently than that of men, or their career aspirations may be taken less seriously than those of men (Correll et al., 2014).

Organizations are not oblivious to the work–family conflicts experienced by employees, especially women. To address the issue of work–family conflict and as attempts to retain high-performing women, many organizations develop policies to help employees balance work and family commitments (Correll et al., 2014). These policies offer employees alternate work arrangements such as flexible work-hours, part-time work, work from home, or paid or unpaid leave. Yet other stresses may manifest themselves for those employees who do take advantage of these policies. Cultural and organizational norms can stigmatize the use of flexibility policies, and this "flexibility stigma" can result in career penalties and negative career outcomes (Blair-Loy, 1999; Correll et al., 2014; Smith and Hatmaker, 2017; Williams et al., 2013). As a result, women leaders may face a "damned if they do, damned if they don't" set of choices with respect to reconciling work and family conflicts. If they take advantage of flexibility policies that are meant to enable their careers, their advancement may stall anyway and they may be further peripheralized or viewed as less serious or committed to the organization. Yet if they put their careers first, they face being labeled as a bad mother (Blair-Loy, 1999; Correll et al., 2014). We must also keep in mind that men also experience a work–family conflict and that their use of flexibility policies goes against cultural norms, but they do not seem to experience the same penalties that women do (Correll et al., 2014).

Our findings also showed different manifestations of gender-exclusive language used in professional settings. Research on gender-exclusive language indicates that it is ostracizing for women (Stout and Dasgupta, 2011). For the local government management profession, gender-exclusive language is yet another discouraging cue that women do not fit the mold of the traditional local government manager. Making leaders aware of the ramifications of their exclusive language is a first step to addressing this issue. Increasing the number of women and women of color at the table is another key step. But neither is necessarily sufficient to changing the stereotypes and cultural expectations that lead to such interactions and reinforce the gender imbalance.

At the heart of the barriers that prevent women from advancing in local government and that serve to maintain a gender imbalance is identity. Local government is not alone or unique in this aspect; women face identity challenges in many settings where men simply do not have to. Often this is the case especially in workplaces or professions where the male worker is the norm, such as in male dominated professions and high-level leadership roles (e.g. Hatmaker, 2014; Roth, 2001). As we saw from our interview participants, in contexts where women challenge the norm, their gender and/or racial identity is often spotlighted or highlighted (Foldy, 2012; Hatmaker, 2013; Kanter, 1977). This attention to women's gender and racial identity acts as a barrier to acceptance into the majority group and to gaining the career, power, and other resource benefits conferred by this belonging. It relegates them to an outsider status from which they must challenge the status quo and negotiate their professional identity to gain legitimacy (Bell and Nkomo, 2000). Women's identity construction at work is complicated by gender stereotypes; men are assumed to possess the traits necessary for leadership and are thus granted a higher status (Ridgeway, 1997, 2001). This automatic status granting advantages men and serves to relegate women to a lower status from which where they must engage in identity work to prove themselves, often over and over (Hatmaker, 2013; Ridgeway, 1997; 2011). Women leaders who are also parents are tasked with constant reconciliation of their professional and parental identity (Smith and Hatmaker, 2017). Women and women of color thus expend a great deal of time negotiating their identity through workplace interactions to move attention away from their identity as a woman or woman of color, wife, or mother (Hatmaker, 2013).

In considering the question of "why so few?" women at the top levels of local government, we might naturally turn to the idea that as the number of women at the top increases, it will spur momentum for more women's advancement. Much of this idea is rooted in Kanter's (1977) work on tokenism that noted that the small numbers of women or members of other subgroups leads to negative effects. These effects include isolation from formal and informal networks, increased performance pressures, and being stereotyped into certain organizational roles (Ely, 1995; Kanter, 1977; Yoder, 1991). Kanter (1977) argued that number balancing was a critical factor toward eliminating these negative effects. And in fact when more women occupy leadership roles they offer role models that can inspire women to aspire to top positions and disprove the idea that being a woman is a liability to advancement (Ibarra, Ely and Kolb, 2013). However, fixing the gender-imbalance issue with an approach rooted solely in numbers balancing has been dispelled as an end-all solution (Ely, 1995; Yoder, 1991). That is, balancing the numbers is not a panacea for the issue of gender imbalance at the top levels of local government and elsewhere. This approach ignores the complexities of structural and cultural norms and expectations that erect barriers for women's advancement and create contexts in which discrimination, harassment, and other interactions serve to maintain the status quo.

Our findings, though limited by sample size, signal that local government management is still in the process of integrating women and people of color into its leadership ranks. Despite gender-imbalanced management being on the radar of researchers and practitioners for upward of forty years, city and county managers are still mostly white and male. This gender imbalance is problematic because it suggests that the local government management profession is drawing from a talent pool that is artificially narrow, to the exclusion of competent, committed, and skilled women and women of color.

7 The Glass Cliff and Gender-Imbalanced Public Sector Leadership

Women continue to be underrepresented in the upper echelons of organizations, an enduring refrain from all corners of society (e.g., Pandey and Amezcua, 2018). Even in public sector organizations, where social equity and diversity are espoused values, women still struggle to reach leadership positions facing persistent barriers as they attempt to build and advance their careers (Riccucci, 2009). A variety of metaphors have been used to draw attention to and explain these seemingly invisible barriers. The *glass ceiling* illustrates that even when women do move up in organizational hierarchies, they still struggle to reach top-level positions (Hymowitz and Shellhardt, 1986; Eagly and Carli, 2007). The *glass escalator* points to the fact that men are often able to advance their careers more quickly than women, even in female-dominated industries (Williams, 1992, 1995). *Glass walls* imply that women strain to attain positions in the higher-paying most influential occupational groups (Miller, Kerr, and Reid, 1999). Finally, a *labyrinth* represents the more complex path women, as compared to men, must navigate in order to move forward in their careers (Eagly and Carli, 2007).

Even the women who do manage to break the ceiling, ride the escalator, scale the walls, and navigate the labyrinth continue to face challenges once they arrive at the top. As a metaphor, the *glass cliff* represents another subtle barrier to women's career advancement – that is, when women do reach the heights of leadership positions, the positions are precarious where the risk of failure is high (Ryan and Haslam, 2005, 2007). Failure in a leadership position can be stigmatizing, resulting in damage to one's reputation, networks, and opportunities, permanently thwarting career advancement (Schepker and Barker, 2018; Sutton and Callahan, 1987). If the leadership positions that women are able to secure have a high risk of failure, women will continue to be disadvantaged in their pursuit of career advancement, organizations will remain predominately male in leadership composition, and public sector organizations, in particular, will be unable to serve diverse populations or pursue social equity, a core public sector value.

We begin this section by defining the glass cliff phenomenon, presenting a synthesis of empirical research, and exploring theoretical explanations for why women may face a glass cliff. Next, we place the glass cliff in the local government management context, posing hypothesis about specific risk factors that should be associated with the appointment of female managers if the glass cliff is a valid explanatory theory. We outline the research design, report the results, and discuss the implications of the results for understanding gender imbalance in public sector leadership.

7.1 The Glass Cliff Phenomenon

Prompted by a news article claiming that organizations suffer financially when women get into leadership positions (Judge, 2003), Michelle K. Ryan and S. Alexander Haslam first conceived the glass cliff phenomenon (2005). In their seminal study, they look not only at company performance *after* women get into leadership, but also at company conditions *before* women get appointed to leadership roles. Ultimately, they refute the causal claim of Judge (2003) and find evidence for what they term the "glass cliff." That is, when women do get into leadership positions, it is in organizations that are already struggling – making such positions precarious with a higher risk of failure (Ryan and Haslam, 2005, 2007).

A glass cliff has been observed in a variety of organizational contexts in multiple countries (see Ryan et al., 2016 and Velte, 2018 for reviews). Similar to the British companies in the first studies by Ryan and Haslam (2005, 2007), US firms that experience a scandal or crisis are more likely to subsequently appoint women to their corporate boards (Brady et al., 2011). The US companies that have weak financial performance are more likely to appoint women to CEO positions (Cook and Glass, 2013; Elsaid and Ursel, 2017). In Sweden, women have increasingly attained leadership positions in higher education administration during a time when such positions are declining in prestige, increasingly onerous, and more difficult to manage while also maintaining scholarly activities (Peterson, 2016).

Though studies are fewer in number, glass cliffs have been observed in public sector organizations also, those in the United States specifically. Women are more likely to be in leadership positions in school districts that must serve populations with diverse needs (Smith, 2015). Women attain leadership positions in US federal regulatory organizations when the work of the agency is more complex and must satisfy competing demands (Smith and Monaghan, 2013). Similarly, conceptualizing failure at the individual level as the intent to leave an organization, Sabharwal (2013) finds that women in the US Senior Executive Service who work in agencies that tend to be dominated by men (see Lowi, 1985 for a description of distributive and constituent agencies) are more likely to experience a glass cliff. Women in these positions report having less influence over policy-making decisions, less empowerment, and more experience with organizational inequities than women in other types of agencies.

While these studies find evidence for the glass cliff phenomenon, findings are not unequivocal with a number of studies finding no evidence of a glass cliff. Data from German and British companies find performance trends prior to the appointment of a female executive are no different than prior to the appointment of a male executive (Bechtoldt, Bannier, and Rock, 2019). Likewise, Santen and Donker (2009) find no association between gender of a director and financial distress among corporate boards in the Netherlands. Some studies even find opposite effects. In Canada, Hennessey, MacDonald, and Carroll (2014) find that women enter corporate board positions when companies are experiencing strong stock market performance, thus meet a "solid ledge" not a glass cliff. Similarly, Adams, Gupta, and Leeth (2009) find that women are appointed to leadership positions in US firms when the firms are in good financial health. Other studies find alternative explanations for the appointment of women to leadership positions. For example, Cook and Glass (2014) find that diversity among decision-makers, not performance of the firm, explains the appointment of women to leadership positions.

Knowledge of the glass cliff adds to our understanding of the persistent gender imbalances in leadership positions around the globe, although this understanding is relatively new having only been explored empirically over the last ten years. While research provides evidence for the existence of a glass cliff, the findings are mixed in both public and private sector settings. Theories about individual and organizational behavior can help to explain why and when a glass cliff may exist. Next, we turn to these theoretical explanations.

7.2 Explanations for the Glass Cliff Phenomenon

As Ryan et al. (2016) note, the glass cliff is not a theory to be proved or disproved, but rather a phenomenon to be explained using existing theory. Theoretical perspectives focusing on the nature of organizations in crisis are useful in understanding when and why women may face a glass cliff when attaining a leadership position.

When an organization is in crisis, people may engage in more risk taking, be more willing to try something different, or "gamble" (Kahneman and Tversky, 1979; Ryan et al., 2016). For example, in a case study of Hurricane Katrina, Boin et al. (2010) find that disaster opens opportunities for challenging the status quo and leaders play a crucial role. Similarly, Sun, Zhu, and Ye (2015) find that boards are more willing to accept a woman as director during times of financial crisis than during times of financial success. Thus, we might expect to find more women in leadership positions when organizations are facing crisis – positioning women precariously.

Organizations in crisis also tend to have more turnover, particularly in leadership positions (Arthaud-Day et al., 2006; Gilson and Vetsuypens, 1993; Ryan et al., 2016; Warner, Watts, and Wruck, 1988). As leaders leave organizations, more opportunities open up for women to secure leadership positions.

Socialization experiences that reinforce gender stereotypes, create social networks, and mentorship may lead men to foresee ample current and/or future leadership opportunities (Ibarra, 1992, 1997, 1999; Schein, 1975; Van Maanen and Schein, 1979). Therefore, accepting a leadership position in a troubled organization may seem both undesirable and unnecessary for a career advancement for men. The same socialization experiences may lead women to expect leadership positions to be rare. Thus, leadership positions in even the most troubled organizations may be seen as an opportunity that must be seized.

Finally, gender stereotypes may make women desirable leaders when an organization is in crisis (Eagly and Carli, 2003; Ryan et al., 2016). Gender stereotypes depict women as communal, collaborative, and understanding (Heilman, 2012). These traits may be seen as suitable for handling an emergency and bringing an organization out of crisis. In other words, we "think crisis, think female" (Ryan et al., 2011). Thus, we would expect women to have a "leadership advantage" in times of organizational crisis (Eagly and Carli, 2003; Vecchio, 2002).

Theory suggests that when organizations face crisis, we can expect women to attain leadership positions, positioning them on a glass cliff where the risk of failure is high. Failure is public, visible, and leaders typically take the blame (Boin et al., 2010; Meindl, Ehrlich, and Dukerich, 1985). In addition, leaders who do not fit the leader prototype tend to be blamed more for failure (Brescoll, Dawson, and Uhlmann, 2010; Eagly and Karau, 2002). If we "think leader, think male" (Hoobler, Wayne, and Lemmon, 2009; Schein, 1975), women leaders will garner harsher blame for failure than their male counterparts (Gupta et al., 2018). If women are more likely to get into these precarious positions, they are more likely to suffer stalled career progress as well. If career progress stalls for women, the upper echelons of organizations will remain homogenous.

While the glass cliff has been considered in a variety of private sector contexts across the globe, less attention has been given to considering the glass cliff in public sector contexts. Unlike private sector settings where profit, price of stock shares, and company survival, can serve as direct measures of risk, public sector settings must use alternatives. As seen in the few studies that do consider the glass cliff in public sector organizations, risk is conceptualized as how hard it is to do the job (complexity), how many people will know if the leader fails (visibility), and whether or not the leader continues employment with the organization (turnover). In the present study, we place the glass cliff in a local government context and focus on aspects of the organizational environment that make management positions "precarious", meaning they challenge the ability of a manager to succeed in their position.

7.3 The Glass Cliff in Local Government Management: Theory and Hypotheses

Local government management is, in some ways, the ideal laboratory for testing for the glass cliff phenomenon. City and county managers have emotionally demanding jobs, sometimes characterized by the political vitriol of elected officials, career instability (managers serve their governing bodies and can be fired at the drop of a hat), and skyrocketing expectations for public service delivery for minimal tax dollars. There is no shortage of gender dynamics, as our interview results convey. We focus on three aspects of a local government organization's environment that create precarious conditions for a manager, challenging their ability to succeed in their positions: political structure, legal liability, and financial performance.

7.3.1 Political Structure

The political structure of a local government can enable or constrain the ability of a local government manager to perform effectively. Municipal governments in the United States tend to assume one of two forms: council-manager and mayor-council (Nelson and Stenberg, 2018). Counties have similar forms of government, the commission-manager is the equivalent of the council-manager form and the county executive form is the equivalent of the mayor-council form in municipalities. In the council-manager form of government, the manager's duties are typically codified in the local government charter and the mayor has less direct power over the manager. By contrast, in mayor-council governments, power is more concentrated in the mayor, giving mayors a more important role in managerial tenure. In strong mayoral forms of government, the mayor can appoint or fire the manager and determine their job functions, making the city or county manager's authority fully dependent on the mayor. Mayors in weak mayoral form of mayor-council government have less power over the manager, but they may exert more influence over managers than mayors in council-manager forms of government. Turnover of mayors has a greater effect on turnover of managers in mayor-council systems (Feiock, Clingermayer, Stream, McCabe, Ahmed, 2001). Also, cities with a mayor elected at-large are less likely to support the sitting city manager than those with mayors selected by council (DeHoog and Whitaker, 1990). Since mayor-council governments are more likely to have a popularly elected mayor (Nelson and Svara, 2010), this also contributes to the likelihood of higher turnover in the mayor-council form of government.

Along with increasing the risk of a manager being fired, mayor-council forms of government politicize the work environment and lead to increased conflict.

Council-manager forms of government privilege good management over politics, in comparison with mayor-council government forms, which incentivize the pursuit of narrow political interests over technical expertise (Feiock and Kim, 2001). In the council manager form, decision-making is distributed across council members, limiting their ability to behave opportunistically; by contrast, mayor-council forms concentrate power in the mayor, enabling him or her to "claim credit for their actions, to reward their friends, and to punish their enemies" (Feiock et al., 2001: 103). Whitaker and DeHoog observed in 1991 the expectation that the council-manager form of government should reduce conflict between the manager and the council by creating clearer lines of authority and precluding the need for the city or county manager to compete with the board. They quote Chester Newland in pointing out "The great strength of council-manager government has been precisely in the combined presence of those two qualities: a powerful council, oriented to community brokerage, and a coordinated executive framework, characterized by diverse expertise and professionalism and free of narrow factionalism" (p. 156).

Given that mayor-council forms of government create greater professional risks in the form of a greater dependency of the manager and a more politicized work environment, we expect that that:

Hypothesis 1. Women will be more likely to be appointed in local governments with mayor-council forms of government than manager-council forms of government.

7.3.2 Legal Liability

The legal liability incurred by a local government organization can challenge a city or county manager's ability to perform effectively. Organizations become liable when they violate laws that seek to align organizational behavior with socially determined edicts (Edelman and Suchman, 1997). For public organizations, the legal environment is one dimension of public sector accountability, which involves the ability of an outside party to levy sanctions or enforce action (Romzek and Dubnick, 1987). When public organizations are subject to sanctions or enforcement, it can create legal risk for both public managers and the organizations they run (Rainey, 2009: 91).

One fertile area of legal risk for public organizations is that of equal employment opportunity, which comprise laws, guidance, regulations, and case law making it illegal to discriminate against job applicants or employees on a range of personal characteristics, including race, age, and sex, among others (Riccucci, 2018). As French notes in his review of discrimination cases at the local government level, an estimated 70 percent of Americans have a protected status under antidiscrimination laws (2009), increasing the likelihood that organizations will violate discrimination law at some point in time.

Discrimination complaints are expensive for organizations, and not just in dollars (see Gelfand et al., 2007, for an overview). On the financial front, investigations of complaints are resource intensive (Hauck, 1997), settlements with complainants can reach the hundreds of millions of dollars (King and Spruell, 2001; James and Wooten, 2006), and stock prices can decline for private firms (Wright, Ferris, Hiller, and Kroll, 1995). In terms of nonmonetary costs, organizations can suffer reputational losses as a result of discrimination lawsuits (Wentling and Palmas-Rivas, 1997), and organizational productivity can erode a result of loss of organizational talent, lower morale, and less organizational capacity (Gelfand et al., 2007). To convey the magnitude of discrimination costs in the United States, consider that the EEOC won $505 million dollars for discrimination complainants in 2018, including awards from state and local government.[13]

The array of monetary and nonmonetary costs posed by discrimination complaints create risks for both local government organizations and their managers. If the glass cliff phenomenon is real, women will be disproportionately located in leadership positions where there has been growth in legal liability issues for the city or county. Thus, we expect that:

Hypothesis 2: Women will be disproportionately located as managers of local government organizations with a history of equal employment opportunity complaints.

7.3.3 Financial Condition

The financial condition of a city or county is another factor that frames success or failure for a chief administrative officer. As Kioko et al. observe, public financial management indicators reflect the manner in which public organizations respond to their environment, interact with stakeholders and make decisions based on risk-reward calculi (2011). The authors note that public financial management is one form of performance management that provides "essential information on organizational outputs and outcomes" (p. 117).

At the local government level, financial condition determines a city or county's ability to recruit and retain employees, deliver quality public services, and buffer itself from economic, social and political shocks (Nelson and Stenberg, 2017). When a local government's financial condition is in decline,

---

[13] www.eeoc.gov/eeoc/statistics/enforcement/index.cfm

it obstructs organizational effectiveness and creates fertile soil for a CAO's voluntary or involuntary exit (DeHoog and Whitaker, 1990). Along these lines, the poverty rate in a community (Feiock et al., 2001) and a decline in a community's per capita personal income (McCabe et al., 2008) have been associated with higher managerial turnover, which is one indication of professional risk in a local government. Thus, we hypothesize:

H3: The weaker financial condition of a city or county will be associated with the appointment of a female CAO.

Because financial condition is such a strong driver of public sector decision-making (Kioko et al., 2011; Rivenbark, Roenigk, and Allison, 2010), we expect it to alter the effects of legal liability and political structure on the likelihood of appointing a woman as CAO. This expectation aligns with local government management research expecting environmental conditions to interact to increase turnover among local government managers (Feiock et al., 2001). In the context of the glass cliff, it stands to reason that financial condition magnifies a governing body's sense of precariousness and further increases the likelihood that women will be appointed as the city or county manager. Accordingly, we hypothesize that:

H4: Financial condition will moderate the likelihood that mayor-council forms of government will result in the appointment of a woman as chief administrator officer.

H4: Financial condition will moderate the likelihood that equal opportunity charges will result in the appointment of a woman as chief administrator officer.

7.4 Testing for the Glass Cliff in Local Government Management: Data and Methods

To test for a glass cliff in local government, we use secondary data on a total of 441 cities and counties in the US state of North Carolina (341 cities and 100 counties). Our dataset was compiled from sources including the University of North Carolina School of Government at Chapel Hill, the US Equal Employment Opportunity Commission, and the North Carolina Local Government Commission. The use of secondary data aligns with much glass cliff research that has relied on financial data on corporations (see Ryan and Haslam, 2007 for an overview).

We use logistic regression models to predict the gender of the local government manager. To examine the glass cliff phenomenon, we include three measures of organizational risk at the local government level – political, legal, and financial. We also include control variables for community diversity, median household income, and population of the local government jurisdiction. Descriptive statistics and bivariate correlations for all measures can be found in Table 5.

Our dependent variable is the gender of the local government manager. This variable is a dichotomous variable where 0 = Male and 1 = Female. (While gender can have more than one category, we had no way of identifying non-binary gender managers). We determined manager gender using membership records from the UNC School of Government as of March 2019, which identifies manager gender for salutation purposes. In our data, 21 percent of cities and 20 percent of counties have a woman in the top manager position, which is slightly above the national average of 17 percent across the nation (ICMA).

Our independent variables seek to capture a local government's political, legal, and financial risk. First, we use form of government to measure political risk. Form of government is coded "1" for the mayor-council form (which is less politically stable and more risky) and "0" for the council-manager form (which is more politically stable and less risky). This data comes from the University of North Carolina Chapel Hill School of Government at Chapel Hill, which tracks form of government for all North Carolinas cities and counties. In our sample, 63 percent of the local governments are governed by the manager-council form, but this percentage masks the fact that all North Carolina counties are manager-council forms of government.

Second, we measure legal risk using Equal Employee Opportunity Commission (EEOC) data on discrimination complaints of age, race, and gender discrimination brought against North Carolina local governments between 1997 and 2016. We requested EEOC data for these discrimination categories because they comprise the vast majority of discrimination complaints. For each of the cities and counties in our sample, we calculate the adjusted group means of EEOC complaints per 1000 residents of the local government jurisdiction ($M = .034$ SD $= .152$)[14].

Finally, we measure financial risk using data on the financial condition of North Carolina local governments drawn from the Local Government

---

[14] We have multilevel data for EEOC complaints and for financial condition; the EEOC and financial condition data are at level 1 whereas the gender of the manager and other county/city are at level 2. We calculated the adjusted group means for the multilevel data using the approach outlined in (Croon and van Veldhoven, 2007). Their approach involves computing *adjusted* group means on the predictor variable and regressing the dependent variable on the adjusted group means. The adjusted group mean for each group is the best linear unbiased predictor (BLUP) of the predictor variable for that group. This is a better approach than a simple mean of prior years' data.

Table 5 Descriptive statistics and correlations

	Mean	SD	1	2	3	4	5	6	7	8	9	10
1 Female (male = 0, female = 1)	0.21	0.41										
2 Unit (county = 0, city = 1)	0.77	0.42	0.01									
3 Community Blau index	0.39	0.19	−0.04	−0.32								
4 Median household income	43464.00	18066.38	0.01	0.05	−0.35							
5 Population	35291.63	98607.45	0.00	−0.37	0.27	0.10						
6 Form of gov (council manager = 0, mayor council = 1)	0.37	0.48	−0.08	0.42	−0.14	0.03	−0.14					
7 EEOC complaints per capita	0.03	0.15	−0.01	0.09	−0.14	0.04	−0.06	−0.02				
8 Operations ratio	1.05	0.08	0.08	0.12	−0.10	0.22	0.01	0.05	−0.03			
9 Fund balance percentage	63.24	80.96	0.03	0.25	−0.14	0.12	−0.13	0.15	−0.01	0.26		
10 Total margin ratio	1.10	0.13	0.01	0.28	−0.19	0.24	−0.12	0.08	0.02	0.46	0.19	
11 Capital assets condition ratio	0.52	0.12	0.16	−0.30	−0.01	0.20	0.15	−0.13	−0.05	0.22	0.00	0.21

Correlations with $p < .05$ arc in bold font

Commission, which oversees financial reporting by the state's cities and counties.[15] We use four indicators of financial condition, given that no one indicator has the potential to capture organizational performance (Kioko, 2011). As Rivenbark, Roenig, and Allison explain (2009), operations ratio, calculated by dividing revenues by expenses, indicates the extent to which a local government lives within its means; the fund balance percent of the general fund represents a local government's solvency; the total margin ratio, calculated by dividing annual revenues by annual expenditures, captures whether a local government is living within its means that year; and the capital assets condition ratio, which measures the useful life left in a jurisdiction's capital assets. For each of the four measures of financial performance we calculated the adjusted group means for three years prior to the appointment of the manager. As Table 5 indicates, the average North Carolina local government lives within its means, as suggested by operations ratios and total margin ratios over "1", and has about 63 percent of its expenses designated for a rainy day and over half the lifespan of its capital assets remaining.

In addition to the independent variables measuring political, legal, and financial risk, we also include several control variables in our models. To measure community diversity we calculate a Blau index of race and ethnicity using the 2010–2014 American Community Survey 5-Year Estimates for each of the cities and counties in our sample.[16] The Blau index is a number ranging from 0 (lacking any racial variation) to 1 (comprising maximum variation for the number of racial categories). In our sample, the average Blau index for cities and counties is 0.39, indicating a moderate level of community diversity on average.

We also control for socioeconomic status and size of the cities and counties in our dataset. Median household income and population size were also obtained from the American Community Survey 5-Year Estimates[17]. The average median household income is over $43,000 and the average population is over 35,000 for the cities and counties in our sample. However, it is important to note, that because counties are comprised of cities, county populations and city populations overlap. The cities in our sample have an average population of 15,500 people while the counties have an average population of 103,000 people.

---

[15] www.nctreasurer.com/slg/lfm/financial-analysis/Pages/Financial-Statistics-Tool.aspx

[16] The Blau index measures variety in a phenomenon and is calculated as 1-the sum of squared proportions comprising each group represented. The data retrieved at American Fact Finder (https://factfinder.census.gov/faces/nav/jsf/pages/index.xhtml) in March 2019. Available racial categories include White, Black or African American, American Indian and Alaska Native, and Asian.

[17] The data retrieved at American Fact Finder (https://factfinder.census.gov/faces/nav/jsf/pages/index.xhtml) in March 2019.

7.4.1 Results of Secondary Data Analysis

We ran hierarchical logistic regression models (Jaccard, 2001) to test the study hypotheses. The hierarchical model allows us to test the following: (1) whether the main effects of the predictor variables significantly improve the model fit over the model with only the control variables and (2) whether the addition of the interaction terms significantly improve the model fit over the model with the main effects and the control variables.

Because coefficients in logistic regression are scale-dependent, we report standardized coefficient to present variables on comparable scales (Aiken and West, 1991; Gelman 2008). As the results in Table 6 show, Model 1 with only the control variables as predictors has the worst fit statistics and is not statistically significant: $\chi^2 = 3.207$, df $= 4$, p $= 0.524$. Model 2 with the main effects of study variables and control variables has improved pseudo R-squared statistics, but is not statistically significant: $\chi^2 = 8.12$, df $= 10$, p $= 0.617$. Model 3 with the main and interaction effects of study variables and control variables has the best model fit statistics: $\chi^2 = 30.596$, df $= 19$, p $= 0.045$.

As the Model 3 results in Table 6 indicate, form of government does not alter the likelihood that women are appointed chief administrative officers, thus contradicting our first hypothesis that mayor-council governments are more politically unstable and thus more likely to hire women from a glass cliff perspective. In terms of legal liability, the odds of having a female manager increases with the number of EEOC complaints per capita for three years prior to the manager's appointment. Thus, women are more likely to land CAO positions when there have been recent legal liability issues, in support of our second hypothesis.

The results for financial condition are mixed. As expected by our third hypothesis, a one standard deviation decrease in the average operations ratio three years prior to a manager's appointment increases by half the odds of appointing a female manager. However, a one standard deviation increase in the three-year average fund balance prior to managerial appointment triples the likelihood that a female CAO is appointed, contradicting the hypothesis. Similarly, a one standard deviation increase in the three-year average capital assets condition ratio prior to appointment more than doubles the odds of a woman being appointed CAO. The average Total Margin Ratio for three years prior to a manager's appointment is not correlated with the gender of the manager, nor are any of the control variables correlated.

Because financial condition is a major driver of decision-making in local government organizations (Kioko, 2011; Rivenbark et al., 2004), we tested the moderating effect of our four measures of financial condition on the

Table 6 Logistic regressions predicting appointment of a female chief administrative officer

Predictor	Model 1				Model 2				Model 3			
	β	p	SE β	Odds ratio	β	p	SE β	Odds ratio	β	p	SE β	Odds ratio
Unit (county = 0, city = 1)	1.037	0.031	0.481	2.820	0.782	0.158	0.554	2.186	0.759	0.224	0.624	2.136
Community Blau index	0.480	0.630	0.996	1.616	0.578	0.565	1.004	1.782	0.609	0.524	0.956	1.839
Median income	0.000	0.117	0.000	1.000	0.000	0.195	0.000	1.000	0.000	0.077	0.000	1.000
Population (log-transformed)	-0.579	0.067	0.316	0.561	-0.617	0.060	0.329	0.540	-0.343	0.310	0.338	0.710
Form of government (council manager = 0, mayor council = 1)					0.229	0.550	0.383	1.257	0.347	0.429	0.438	1.414
EEOC complaints per capita[a]					-0.081	0.616	0.162	0.922	1.411	0.023	0.622	4.100
Operations ratio[a]					-0.106	0.658	0.239	0.900	-0.624	0.089	0.366	0.536
Fund balance percentage[a]					0.047	0.785	0.172	1.048	1.122	0.055	0.585	3.072
Total margin ratio[a]					0.103	0.716	0.283	1.108	-0.300	0.432	0.382	0.740
					0.346	0.062	0.185	1.413	0.440	0.071	0.243	1.553

	B	S.E.	p	Exp(B)
Capital assets condition ratio[a]				
EEOC complaints per capita × Operations ratio[b]	0.418	0.451	0.555	1.518
EEOC complaints per capita × Fund Balance %[b]	1.159	0.015	0.477	3.186
EEOC complaints per capita × Total margin ratio[b]	−1.133	0.011	0.445	0.322
EEOC complaints per capita × Capital assets condition ratio[b]	−0.094	0.789	0.352	0.910
Form of government × Operations ratio[b]	0.306	0.404	0.367	1.358
Form of government × Fund balance[b]	−1.090	0.040	0.530	0.336
Form of government × Total margin ratio[b]	0.545	0.206	0.431	1.724
Form of government × Capital assets condition ratio[b]	−0.206	0.340	0.216	0.814
χ^2	6.606 (0.158)	11.74 (0.303)	28.667 (0.052)	

Table 6 (cont.)

Predictor	Model 1				Model 2				Model 3			
	ß	p	SE ß	Odds ratio	ß	p	SE ß	Odds ratio	ß	p	SE ß	Odds ratio
df	4				10				18			
−2 Log likelihood	251.347				246.214				229.276			
Cox & Snell R Square	0.026				0.045				0.106			
Nagelkerke R Square	0.040				0.071				0.167			

[a] standardized z-scores used in regression model

[b] standardized z-scores for each product term of centered raw scores used in regression model

relationships between political structure and discrimination charges on the appointment of a female manager. The interactions yielded three significant relationships out of eight total: an increase in the fund balance percentage renders significant the positive influence of form of government on the appointment of a female manager ($p = 0.04$); an increase in the fund balance magnifies the relationship between equal employment opportunity complaints per capita and the appointment of a female manager ($p < 0.02$); and an increase in the total margins ratio intensifies the relationship between equal employment opportunity complaints per capita and the appointment of a female manager ($p < 0.02$). Thus, our fourth and fifth hypotheses are contradicted, as they run in the opposite direction that we expected: stronger, not weaker, financial condition magnifies the effects of legal liability and political structure on the appointment of a female CAO.

7.4.2 Discussion of Secondary Data Analysis

The glass cliff refers to the theoretically greater likelihood that women will be appointed to precarious leadership positions (Ryan and Haslam, 2005). While the glass cliff phenomenon has been detected in a range of mostly private sector contexts (Ryan et al., 2016), it has received less attention in public sector contexts. While the exact drivers of the glass cliff phenomenon are not precisely known, some possibilities include organizational crises that lead hiring authorities to give women a chance (benevolent sexism) (Ryan and Haslam, 2007) or choose women for a much-needed infusion of (what they assume will be) feminine leadership styles (Bruckmuller et al., 2014). Another possibility is that women seize leadership opportunities than men will not take (Ryan and Haslam, 2007), either relishing the challenge and seeing opportunities to enact positive change (Ashby, Ryan, and Haslam, 2007) or taking advantage of scarce leadership opportunities.

In the context of local government management, we conceptualize precariousness as professional risk for local government managers and define risk as the characteristics of a local government organization that lowers a manager's likelihood of succeeding in their position. We used hierarchical logistic regression to predict the gender of the manager based on three aspects of professional risk in local government management: legal liability, political structure, and financial performance.

Our analysis suggests that the government structure – mayor-council form or council-manager form – does not influence the appointment of a female manager. This contradicted our first hypothesis that women would more likely be concentrated in mayor-council forms of government, where power is concentrated in the mayor, governance is more politicized, and the prospect of internal conflict is greater. Two explanations underlie the finding that form of government does not influence the gender of managerial appointment. First, if there is a glass cliff in local government management, political structure does not capture it. Rather, all politics are local and affect forms of government equally. A second possibility is that our sample of 341 cities and 100 counties excludes several hundred very small jurisdictions for which data were not available, where women may be more likely to serve as chief administrative officers, thus we are missing critical data that could have changed our results.

With regard to legal liability, women are more likely to serve as local government managers in cities or counties where EEOC complaints are higher in the three years prior to their appointment. This finding supports our second hypothesis and provides evidence for the existence of a glass cliff phenomenon. Drawing on just one theoretical explanation for the glass cliff, it could be that lawsuits around social injustice – complaints that the organization has broken laws around age, gender, and race discrimination – trigger the need for a local government to project a significant cultural change in the organization (Ashby, Ryan and Haslam, 2007). Or it could be that lawsuits trigger the perceived need for more feminine leadership compared with the more hierarchical, competitive, and rigid cultures that can trigger lawsuits (Rawski and Workman-Stark, 2018).

The mixed effects of financial performance on the appointment of a female manager, addressed by our third hypothesis, are puzzling. That a lower operations ratio correlates with the appointment of a female manager is consistent with the glass cliff and suggests weaker financial performance. However, two measures of stronger financial performance, fund balance percentage and capital assets condition ratio, are associated with a higher likelihood of a female manager. The seeming contradiction in these measures may point toward a short-term vs. long-term distinction: perhaps women are appointed under conditions of longer-term financial health – required to build a fund balance and take care of capital assets – but short-term spending. If so, these findings contradict the glass cliff and, rather, suggest a "solid ledge" similar to that found by Hennessey, MacDonald, and Carroll (2014) and Adams, Gupta, and Leeth (2009).

Financial conditions also sometimes magnify the effects of political structure and legal liability on the likelihood of appointing a female CAO, although in the opposite direction expected by our fourth and fifth hypotheses. Mayor-council government forms are more likely to appoint a female CAO when the fund balance is higher. A higher fund balance also further strengthens the likelihood that jurisdictions with more EEOC complaints will appoint a female CAO. Perhaps flush resources provide local governments with the resources needed to consider a broader talent pool. Alternatively, a broader talent pool may be drawn to leadership positions with more resources.

All in all, our analyses point to a legal glass cliff for women in North Carolina local government organizations, but not political or financial glass cliffs. But there are limits to conclusions from this finding because it is not clear, from this research or existing studies, whether the glass cliff has positive, negative, or mixed effects for women in leadership positions. If women are appointed as chief administrative officers under conditions of legal liability and make public sector organizations more just and effective, then it could be that tackling such challenges is a career boon. Our data also cannot speak to whether patterns of appointments are due to features of the local government that lead women to apply, hiring preferences of the governing body, or some combination of both. Are women drawn to challenges? Do challenges in the operating environment lead governing bodies to favor women for a mix of sexist and hopeful reasons? Future research is ripe with opportunity to tackle these questions, as doing so will shed light on the glass cliff as another form of gender discrimination or a turning point in opportunities for women in public sector leadership positions.

8 Discussion, Highlights, and Conclusions

This research sought to explore factors that account for gender imbalance in public service leadership, focusing on local government management as our laboratory. Gender imbalance in the public sector is a pernicious problem that transcends all levels of government (DeHart-Davis et al., 2018). We focused on local government management because it is the unit of government that interacts most closely with citizens, has a wide array of service delivery functions, and has been led by mostly white men since its inception in 1908 (Nelson and Stenberg, 2018).

We employed a problem-centered approach to explore gender-imbalanced local government management, which draws on multiple theories to identify a range of interim mechanisms driving a social phenomenon (Davis and Marquis, 2005). Along with multiple theories, we used multiple data sources and methods for detecting the factors underlying gender-imbalanced leadership. A historical overview of local government management reveals a professional field that has been exceedingly slow to integrate women, despite a recognition since the 1970s that women were woefully underrepresented in the managerial ranks. Interviews with thirty female local government managers surfaced patterns of comments that suggest why women decide to pursue (or not pursue) the top position and the challenges to serving as a manager once they are hired. A sequence analysis of forty-one resumes reveals two career paths to local government management for which women and men differ. And using the glass cliff concept as a guiding framework, we analyzed secondary data to test whether female managers of North Carolina local governments were more likely to be appointed in jurisdiction where legal, political, and financial risks were high. In this section, we look across these findings to identify highlights and draw conclusions for understanding gender imbalance and public service leadership more generally.

8.1 Highlights of the Research

The history of women in local government management suggests that path dependency might be the biggest barrier to increasing the number of women in top city and county management positions. Path-dependency theory argues that the strongest predictor of tomorrow is yesterday, unless the conditions that created current circumstances change (Pierson, 2000). In absence of large shocks to any social system, circumstances change slowly (Greener, 2005). The history of women in local government management confirms this. More than thirty years since ICMA first released statistics estimating that only 13 percent of local government managers were women, that figure is now only 6 percent higher. Furthermore, many of the patterns identified in ICMA's first task force for women were repeated in the second task force for women thirty years later (including selection by mostly male elected officials, the protégé (or "good old boy") system; female stereotypes; and lack of upward mobility assignments for women. While local government management may pose a negative path dependency, other countries have had success with positive path dependencies around gender, such as quota policies to increase the number of women on corporate boards in Norway and in Spain (Terjesen, Aguilera, and Lorenz, 2015). The implication for gender balance in public service generally, and local government management particularly, is that it will take a large shock to the system, in the form of proactive and aggressive recruitment practices combined with an increase in the number of women willing to pursue top positions to tip the scales toward gender-balanced leadership.

The thirty interviews conducted with women working in local government management, either at the top or at the second level, reveal experiences of being visible in some ways and invisible in others, what Roberts and colleagues calls the "double-edged sword of visibility" (2018). Female managers – and female managers of color, in particular – become visible because they are something "other" than white men, the cultural dominant in the local government management profession. Female managers stand out, at managers conferences, in council meetings and ribbon cutting ceremonies. While this visibility could be construed as beneficial, it more often created additional challenge for our interview participants not faced by men, in the form of higher scrutiny, greater stereotyping, and additional pressures to prove one's self. But female managers can also be rendered invisible when gendered language ignores the fact that there's a female in the room and social networking opportunities are closed off, explicitly or implicitly.

Our analysis of the resumes of forty-one city and county managers in North Carolina reveal gender differences in career paths. Nearly 90 percent of the women in the sample had started their careers in local government and half were promoted from within their organizations to the county manager position (compared with only a quarter in the male sample). None had prior private sector experience, compared with over half the male sample. They are nearly identical in average years in the workforce, in public service, and their current position, although it took the women three years longer on average to get to the top position. Thus, most of the female county managers fell into the traditionalist career path, lifers who work their way up in their city or county, accumulate considerable local government experience and social capital along the way, and tend to hold graduate degrees (mostly MPAs). By contrast, protean career paths were dominated by men, with more checkered career paths: more likely to work in the private sector, not starting out in local government, and with less than a quarter having MPA degrees. This result is consistent with research by Smith, Hatmaker, and Subedi that women in federal leadership positions also pursue more traditional career paths, with deeper, fewer network ties and more specialized expertise (2015).

Several patterns from interview data shed light on the pursuit of traditional over protean careers for women in local government management. The finding that women tend to rise through the ranks within local government organizations is consistent with interview findings that family and work–life balance are primary considerations for women in deciding to pursue or not to pursue top management positions. Changing jobs geographically, the golden strategy for ascending in local government management, is much harder for women to pull off given historically disproportionate caregiving responsibilities (Stivers, 2002). Greater caregiving responsibilities generally make women less professionally mobile, opting instead for the long game that allows more stability in their personal lives. Our interview findings also suggest that heightened scrutiny and the self-imposed pressure to perform might drive the pursuit of traditional over protean career paths, to counteract the long odds of succeeding in a male-dominated profession (Barbulescu and Bidwell, 2012).

Our final analysis tested for the effect of a glass cliff in the appointment of women as North Carolina local government managers. The glass cliff refers to the theoretically greater likelihood that women will be appointed to precarious leadership positions. While the glass cliff phenomenon has been detected in a range of mostly private sector contexts (see Ryan et al., 2016), it has received less attention in public sector contexts. If the glass cliff exists in public service leadership positions, it threatens to set in motion a cycle of failure by which women disproportionately join professionally risky organizations, are personally blamed for failures when circumstances go awry, and fall further behind in career opportunities as a result.

In the context of local government management, we conceptualize precariousness as professional risk for local government managers and define risk as the characteristics of a local government organization that lowers a manager's likelihood of succeeding in their position. We used hierarchical logistic regression to predict the gender of the manager based on three aspects of professional risk in local government management: legal liability, political structure, and financial performance. Our analysis suggests that the government structure – mayor-council form or manager-council form – does not influence the appointment of a female manager when considering a wide range of other influences. This contradicted our expectation that women would more likely be concentrated in mayor-council forms of government, where power is concentrated in the mayor, governance is more politicized, and the prospect of internal conflict is greater. Financial performance exerted mixed effects on the appointment of a female manager, but in the opposite direction: either no effect was detected or positive financial performance correlated with the appointment of a female manager. Legal liability was the only glass cliff effect detected, observed in correlation between discrimination complaints filed with the EEOC three years prior to a manager's appointment and the gender of the manager. This finding supports the glass cliff explanation that female leaders will be chosen when there is a need to demonstrate cultural change via a break from prior practices.

8.2 Conclusions

Looking across these strands of research, we return to our original intent of conducting problem-driven research and the assumption that gender-balanced research is inherently and normatively good for society. These assumptions thus beg us to look across our research findings to paint a fuller portrait of gender-imbalanced public service leadership and identify what can and cannot be done to rectify it.

One conceptual anchor for our findings can be found in the idea of the career labyrinth described by Eagly and Carli (2007). Pathways to top leadership for women are complex, obscure, and more difficult to navigate than the same paths for men. Like Eagly's research subjects, the women in our sample face biases that challenge their authority and legitimacy for leadership positions, must cope with the gender stereotypes associated with leadership style, and navigate societal pressures to be both committed to family as well as work. These obstacles, both implicit and explicit, impede their professional trajectories. Perhaps as a result, women pursue traditional career paths, focusing on one organization or sector, going above and beyond to repeatedly demonstrate their competence, knowledge, skills, and social capital in order to advance, even if slowly, on their career paths. In the pursuit of career advancement, women may join organizations that need their femininity to project cultural change, a new type of leader to demonstrate that the organization is not unjust after all. And some must navigate these challenges all while pursuing a balanced life so that they can attend to family commitments and society's expectation that they be nurturing and compassionate caregivers. These challenges are exhausting, energy-depleting, and a source of competitive advantage for male public service leaders who are largely exempt from these experiences.

Given the pernicious and persistent nature of gender-imbalanced public sector leadership generally – and local government management in particular – what are the potential solutions? If we assume that gender-imbalanced public service leadership is a path-dependent phenomenon, then it will require a significant shock to the social system to increase in the number of women who are willing to pursue top-level positions (Greener, 2005). One such shock might come in form of an increasing number of women holding elected office and thus encouraging a pink wave in government that encourages the pursuit of top positions.

Another possibility is that local government management associations will pursue a concerted effort to make men more aware of the experiences of women in local government management and thus more likely to interrupt the behavioral patterns – of themselves and others – that perpetuate cycles of exclusion. At the local government management level, the cherished golf tournament employed by many professional associations must be balanced with non-gendered opportunities for social networking; male city and county managers can be encouraged to eschew gender-exclusive language and informal socializing that leave women out of important professional opportunities; and state and national associations can address work–life balance as a professional culture issues that will continue to discourage women based on the false impression that local government managers must choose between family and work.

Along with these interventions, more engaged research is needed to understand the true talent pool for public sector leadership. As it currently stands, the low percentage of women in public sector leadership positions suggest an artificially narrow talent pool, due to a possible combination of women and people of color (1) not applying for these positions, (2) applying but not being chosen, or (3) leaving the public sector altogether. These possibilities suggest the need for surveys to identify career plans of prospective public sector leaders, cooperative data collection with search firms to estimate the gender of job applicants, and public management scholars interested in gender-imbalanced public sector leadership to track the career movements of public sector leaders at the local, state, and federal levels.

While our research has focused on local government management, it holds implications for broader public sector leadership. Areas of public service that have been historically male-dominated will introduce path dependencies that make achieving gender-balanced leadership a challenge, but not insurmountably so. Public sector careers that are time-intensive must indoctrinate members to the importance of work–life balance for achieving diversity in leadership, as the two go hand in hand and should not be either-or scenarios. Overcoming experiences of exclusion and social isolation by female leaders can be easily fixed: greater awareness of these experiences by male leaders, who can commit to using gender-inclusive language and opening up social networking opportunities. Finally, there can be a greater recognition that gender-balanced leadership reaps a whole host of benefits for the public sector: it conveys social equity to citizens, produces leaders with a more holistic view of the world, and symbolizes social equity, so that no one type of person holds disproportionate power societally. In other words, gender-balanced leadership is a matter of public value and should be pursued accordingly.

References

Abbott, A. (1995). "Sequence Analysis: New Methods for Old Ideas." *Annual Review of Sociology* 21 (1): 93–113. https://doi.org/10.1146/annurev.so.21.080195.000521

Acker, J. (1990). "Hierarchies, Jobs, Bodies: A Theory of Gendered Organization." *Gender & Society* 4 (2): 139–158. https://doi.org/10.1177/089124390004002002

Adams, S. M., Gupta, A., & Leeth, J. D. (2009). "Are Female Executives Over-Represented in Precarious Leadership Positions?" *British Journal of Management* 20 (1): 1–12.

Aiken, L. S., West, S. G., & Reno, R. R. (1991). *Multiple Regression: Testing and Interpreting Interactions*. Newbury Park, CA: Sage Publications.

Antil, P., Letourneau, T., & Cameron, A. (2014). "Final Report on the Status of Women in the Profession." Washington, DC: International City/County Management Association (ICMA). https://icma.org/sites/default/files/306859_Task%20Force%20on%20Women%20in%20the%20Profession%20Final%20Report%202014.pdf

Arthaud-Day, M. L., Certo, S. T., Dalton, C. M., & Dalton, D. R. (2006). "A Changing of the Guard: Executive and Director Turnover Following Corporate Financial Restatements." *Academy of Management Journal* 49 (6): 1119–1136.

Arthur, M. B. & Rosseau, D. M. (1996). *The Boundaryless Career: A New Employment Principle for a New Organizational Era*. New York: Oxford University Press.

Avery, D. R. (2003). "Reactions to Diversity in Recruitment Advertising: Are Differences Black and White?" *Journal of Applied Psychology* 88 (4): 672–679. https://doi.org/10.1037/0021-9010.88.4.672

Barbulescu, R. & Bidwell, M. (2012). "Do Women Choose Different Jobs from Men? Mechanisms of Application Segregation in the Market for Managerial Workers." *Organization Science* 24 (3): 737–756. https://doi.org/10.1287/orsc.1120.0757

Bechtoldt, M. N., Bannier, C. E., & Rock, B. (2019). "The Glass Cliff Myth? Evidence from Germany and the U.K." *The Leadership Quarterly, Advanced Online Publication*. https://doi.org/10.1016/j.leaqua.2018.11.004

Becker, G. S. (1993). *Human Capital*. Chicago: University of Chicago Press.

Becker, G. (2019). *Human Capital*. www.econlib.org/library/Enc/HumanCapital.html

Bell, E. L. J. E. & Nkomo, S. M. (2001). *Our Separate Ways: Black and White Women and the Struggle for Professional Identity.* Boston: Harvard Business School Press.

Blair-Loy, M. (1999). "Career Patterns of Executive Women in Finance: An Optimal Matching Analysis." *American Journal of Sociology* 104 (5): 1346–1397.

Boin, A., Hart, P. T., McConnell, A., & Preston, T. (2010). "Leadership Style, Crisis Response and Blame Management: The Case of Hurricane Katrina." *Public Administration* 88 (3): 706–723.

Borgatti, S. P. & Foster, P. C. (2003). "The Network Paradigm in Organizational Research: A Review and Typology." *Journal of Management* 29 (6): 991–1013.

Bowling, C. J., Kelleher, C. A., Jones, J., & Wright, D. S. (1970). "Cracked Ceilings, Firmer Floors, and Weakening Walls: Trends and Patterns in Gender Representation among Executives Leading American State Agencies." *Public Administration Review* 66 (6): 823–836.

Bowling, C. J., Kelleher, C. A., Jones, J., & Wright, D. S. (2006). "Cracked Ceilings, Firmer Floors, and Weakening Walls: Trends and Patterns in Gender Representation among Executives Leading American State Agencies, 1970–2000." *Public Administration Review* 66 (6): 823–836. https://doi.org/10.1111/j.1540–6210.2006.00651.x

Boynton, R. & Deil, W. (1971). "Mayor-Manager Relationships in Large Council-Manager Cities: A Reinterpretation." *Public Administration Review* 31 (1): 28–36.

Brady, D., Issacs, K., Reeves, M., Burroway R., & Reynolds, M. (2011). "Sector, Size, Stability, and Scandal: Explaining the Presence of Female Executives in Fortune 500 Firms." *Gender in Management: An International Journal* 26 (1): 84–104.

Brass, D. J. (1995). "A Social Network Perspective on Human Resources Management." In G. R. Ferris (ed.), *Research in Personnel and Human Resources Management* (pp. 39–79). Greenwich, CT: JAI Press.

Brems, C. & Johnson, M. E. (1990). "Reexamination of the Bem Sex-Role Inventory: The Interpersonal BSRI." *Journal of Personality Assessment* 55 (3–4): 484–498.

Brescoll, V. L., Dawson, E., & Uhlmann, E. L. (2010). "Hard Won and Easily Lost: The Fragile Status of Leaders in Gender-Stereotype-Incongruent Occupations." *Psychological Science* 21 (11): 1640–1642. https://doi.org/10.1177/0956797610384744

Breslin, R. A., Pandey, S., & Riccucci, N. M. (2017). "Intersectionality in Public Leadership Research: A Review and Future Research Agenda."

Review of Public Personnel Administration 37 (2): 160–182. https://doi
.org/10.1177/0734371X17697118

Bruckmüller, S., Ryan, M. K., Rink, F., & Haslam, S. A. (2014). "Beyond the
Glass Ceiling: The Glass Cliff and Its Lessons for Organizational Policy."
Social Issues and Policy Review 8 (1): 202–223.

Brzinsky-Fay, C., Kohler, U., & Lunaik, M. (2006). "Sequence Analysis with
Stata." *The Stata Journal* 6 (4): 435–460.

Buckwalter, D. W. & Parsons, R. J. (2000). *Local City Managers Career Paths:
Which Way to the Top?* The Municipal Yearbook 2000. Washington, DC:
International City/County Managers Association.

Burke, S. & Collins, K. M. (2001). "Gender Differences in Leadership Styles
and Management Skills." *Women in Management Review* 16 (5):
244–257.

Burns, R. A. (1980). "Women in Municipal Management: Choice, Challenge
and Change." RIE 220370. New Brunswick, NJ: Rutgers University.
https://eric.ed.gov/?id=ED220370

Carpenter, D. P. (1996). "Corporate Identity and Administrative Capacity in
Executive Departments." Dissertation, Chicago: University of Chicago.
https://books.google.com/books/about/Corporate_Identity_and_Administ
rative_Ca.html?id=JQPWNwAACAAJ

Cassell, J. (1998). *The Woman in the Surgeon's Body.* Cambridge: Harvard
University Press.

Catalyst (Organization). (2004). *The Bottom Line: Connecting Corporate
Performance and Gender Diversity.* New York: Catalyst.

Catalyst. (2019). "Quick Take: Women in the Workforce – United States." www
.catalyst.org/research/women-in-the-workforce-united-states/

Collinson, D. L. & Hearn, J. (1996). *Men as Managers, Managers as Men:
Critical Perspectives on Men, Masculinities and Managements.* Thousand
Oaks, CA: Sage Publications.

Cook, A. & Glass, C. (2013). "Glass Cliffs and Organizational Saviors: Barriers
to Minority Leadership in Work Organizations?" *Social Problems* 60 (2):
168–187.

Cook, A. & Glass, C. (2014). "Above the Glass Ceiling: When Are Women and
Racial/Ethnic Minorities Promoted to CEO?" *Strategic Management
Journal* 35 (7): 1080–1089.

Correll, S. J., Kelly, E. L., O'Connor, L. T., & Williams, J. C. (2014).
"Redesigning, Redefining Work." *Work and Occupations* 41 (1): 3–17.

Correll, S. J. & Ridgeway, C. L. (2003). *Expectation States Theory. In
Delamater, J., (ed.) Handbook of Social Psychology.* New York: Kluwer
Academic Publishers.

Croon, M. A. & van Veldhoven, M. J. M. (2007). "Predicting Group-Level Outcome Variables from Variables Measured at the Individual Level: A Latent Variable Multilevel Model." *Psychological Methods* 12 (1): 45–57.

Davies, A. R. & Frink, B. D. (2014). "The Origins of the Ideal Worker: The Separation of Work and Home in the United States from the Market Revolution to 1950." *Work and Occupations* 41 (1): 18–39.

Davis, G. F. & Marquis, C. (2005). "Prospects for Organization Theory in the Early Twenty-First Century: Institutional Fields and Mechanisms." *Organization Science* 16 (4): 332–343. https://doi.org/10.1287/orsc.1050.0137

DeHart-Davis, L., Hatmaker, D. M., Oberfield, Z. W., & Smith, A. E. (2018). "Public Sector Diversity Research: Taking Stock." In Stazyk, E. C. & Frederickson, H. G. (eds.) *Handbook of American Public Administration*. Northampton, MA: Edward Elgar Publishing, 277–288.

DeHoog, R. H. & Whitaker, G. P. (1990). "Political Conflict or Professional Advancement: Alternative Explanations of City Manager Turnover." *Journal of Urban Affairs* 12 (4): 361–377.

DeHoog, R. & Whitaker, G. (1991). "City Managers under Fire: How Conflict Leads to Turnover." *Public Administration Review* 51 (1): 156. https://doi.org/0.2307/977109

Duehr, E. E. & Bono, J. E. (2006). "Men, Women, and Managers: Are Stereotypes Finally Changing?" *Personnel Psychology* 59 (4): 815–846.

Eagly, A. & Carli, L. L. (2007). "Women and the Labyrinth of Leadership." *Harvard Business Review* 85 (9): 63–71.

Eagly, A. H. & Carli, L. L. (2003). "The Female Leadership Advantage: An Evaluation of the Evidence." *The Leadership Quarterly* 14 (6): 807–834. https://doi.org/10.1016/j.leaqua.2003.09.004

Eagly, A. H. & Johnson, B. T. (1990). "Gender and Leadership Style: A Meta-analysis." *Psychological Bulletin* 108 (2): 233.

Eagly, A. H. & Karau, S. J. (2002). "Role Congruity Theory of Prejudice toward Female Leaders." *Psychological Review* 109 (3): 573–598.

Eagly, A. H. & Kite, M. E. (1987). "Are Stereotypes of Nationalities Applied to Both Women and Men?" *Journal of Personality and Social Psychology* 53 (3): 451.

Eagly, A. H., Makhijani, M. G., & Klonsky, B. G. (1992). "Gender and the Evaluation of Leaders: A Meta-analysis." *Psychological Bulletin* 111 (1): 3–22.

Edelman, L. & Suchman, M. C. (1997). "The Legal Environments of Organizations." *Annual Review of Sociology* 23 (1): 479–515.

Elsaid, E. & Ursel, N. C. (2017). "Re-Examining the Glass Cliff Hypothesis Using Survival Analysis: The Case of Female CEO Tenure." *British Journal of Management* 29 (1): 156–170.

Ely, R. J. (1995). "The Power in Demography: Women's Social Constructions of Gender Identity at Work." *Academy of Management Journal* 38 (3): 589–634. https://doi.org/10.5465/256740

Ernst and Young (2017). *Think Governments Are Achieving Gender Diversity in the Workforce? Think Again.* New York: Ernst and Young.

Feeney, M. & Stritch, J. (2019). "Family-Friendly Policies, Gender, and Work–Life Balance in the Public Sector." *Review of Public Personnel Administration* 39 (3): 442–448.

Feiock, R. C., Clingermayer, J. C., Stream, C., McCabe, B. C., & Ahmed, S. (2001). "Political Conflict, Fiscal Stress, and Administrative Turnover in American Cities." *State and Local Government Review* 33 (2): 101–108.

Feiock, R. C. & Kim, J. H. (2001). "Form of Government, Administrative Organization, and Local Economic Development Policy." *Journal of Public Administration Research and Theory* 11 (1): 29–50.

Feiock, R. E. & Stream, G. (1998). "Explaining the Tenure of Local Government Managers." *Journal of Public Administration Research and Theory* 8 (1): 117–130.

Foldy, E. G. (2012). "Something of Collaborative Manufacture: The Construction of Race and Gender Identities in Organizations." *The Journal of Applied Behavioral Science* 48 (4): 495–524. https://doi.org/10.1177/0021886312440041

Fox, R. & Schuhmann, R. (1999). "Gender and Local Government: A Comparison of Women and Men City Managers." *Public Administration Review* 59 (3): 231–242. https://doi.org/10.2307/3109951

French, P. E. (2009). *Employment Laws and the Public Sector Employer: Lessons to Be Learned from a Review of Lawsuits Filed against Local Governments. Public Administration Review* 69 (1): 92–103.

Gelfand, M. J., Nishii, L. H., Raver, J. L., & Schneider, B. (2007). Discrimination in Organizations: An Organizational-Level Systems Perspective (CAHRS Working Paper# 07–08).

Gelman, A. (2008). "Scaling Regression Inputs by Dividing by Two Standard Deviations." *Statistics in Medicine* 27 (15): 2865–2873.

Germain, M. L., Herzog, M. J. R., & Hamilton, P. R. (2012). "Women Employed in Male-Dominated Industries: Lessons Learned from Female Aircraft Pilots, Pilots-in-Training and Mixed-Gender Flight Instructors." *Human Resource Development International* 15 (4): 435–453.

Gilson, S. C. & Vetsuypens, M. R. (1993). "CEO Compensation in Financially Distressed Firms: An Empirical Analysis." *Journal of Finance* 48 (2): 425–458.

Greener, I. (2005). "The Potential of Path Dependence in Political Studies." *Politics* 25 (1): 62–72. https://doi.org/10.1111/j.1467–9256.2005.00230.x

Gubler, M., Arnold, J., & Coombs, C. (2014). "Reassessing the Protean Career Concept: Empirical Findings, Conceptual Components, and Measurement." *Journal of Organizational Behavior* 35 (1): 23–40.

Gupta, V. K., Han, S., Mortal, S. C., & Silveri, S. D. (2018). "Do Women CEOs Face Greater Threat of Shareholder Activism Compared to Male CEOs? A Role Congruity Perspective." *Journal of Applied Psychology* 103 (2): 228–236.

Guy, M. E. & Meier, K. J. (2016). *Women and Men of the States: Public Administrators and the State Level.* Armonk, NY: Taylor and Francis.

Guy, M. E. & Newman, M. A. (2004). "Women's Jobs, Men's Jobs: Sex Segregation and Emotional Labor." *Public Administration Review* 64 (3): 289–298.

Hall, D. T. (1976). *Careers in Organizations.* Santa Monica, CA: Goodyear Publishing Company.

Hall, D. T. (2004). "The Protean Career: A Quarter-Century Journey." *Journal of Vocational Behavior* 65: 113.

Haslam, S. A. & Ryan, M. K. (2008). "The Road to the Glass Cliff: Differences in the Perceived Suitability of Men and Women for Leadership Positions in Succeeding and Failing Organizations." *The Leadership Quarterly* 19 (5): 530–546. https://doi.org/10.1016/j.leaqua.2008.07.011

Hatmaker, D. M. (2013). "Engineering Identity: Gender and Professional Identity Negotiation among Women Engineers." *Gender, Work & Organization* 20 (4): 382–396.

Hatmaker, D. M. & Park, H. H. (2014). "Who Are All These People? Longitudinal Changes in New Employee Social Networks within a State Agency." *The American Review of Public Administration* 44 (6): 718–739.

Hazel, M. & Nurius, P. (1986). "Possible Selves." *American Psychologist* 41: 954–969.

Heilman, M. E. (2001). "Description and Prescription: How Gender Stereotypes Prevent Women's Ascent up the Organizational Ladder." *Journal of Social Issues* 57: 657–674.

Heilman, M. E. (2012). "Gender Stereotypes and Workplace Bias." *Research in Organizational Behavior* 31: 113–135.

Hennessey, S. M., MacDonald, K., & Carroll, W. (2014). "Is There a Glass Cliff or a Solid Ledge for Female Appointees to the Board of Directors?" *Journal of Organizational Culture, Communications and Conflict* 18 (2): 125–139.

Higgins, M. C. & Kram, K. E. (2001). "Reconceptualizing Mentoring at Work: A Developmental Network Perspective." *Academy of Management Review* 26 (2): 264–288.

Herring, C. (2009). "Does Diversity Pay? Race, Gender, and the Business Case for Diversity." *American Sociological Review* 74 (2): 208–224.

Hoobler, J. M., Wayne, S. J., & Lemmon, G. (2009). "Bosses' Perceptions of Family Work Conflict and Women's Promotability: Glass Ceiling Effects." *Academy of Management Journal* 52 (5): 939–957.

Hulett, D. M., Bendick Jr, M., Thomas, S. Y., & Moccio, F. (2008). "Enhancing Women's Inclusion in Firefighting in the USA." International Journal of Diversity in *Organisations, Communities & Nations* 8 (2): 189–207.

Hutchinson, J., Walker, E., & McKenzie, F. H. (2014). "Leadership in Local Government: 'No Girls Allowed.'" *Australian Journal of Public Administration* 73 (2): 181–191.

Hymowitz, C. & Schellhardt, T. D. (1986). "The Glass-Ceiling: Why Women Can't Seem to Break the Invisible Barrier that Blocks them from Top Jobs." *The Wall Street Journal* 24 (1): 1573–1592.

Ibarra, H. (1992). "Homophily and Differential Returns: Sex Differences in Network Structure and Access in an Advertising Firm." *Administrative Science Quarterly* 37 (3): 422–447. https://doi.org/10.2307/2393451

(1997). "Paving an Alternative Route: Gender Differences in Managerial Networks." *Social Psychology Quarterly* (March 1) 91–102.

(1999). "Provisional Selves: Experimenting with Image and Identity in Professional Adaptation." *Administrative Science Quarterly* 44 (4): 764–791.

Ibarra, H., Ely, R., & Kolb, D. (2013). "Women Rising: The Unseen Barriers." *Harvard Business Review* 91 (9): 60–66.

Ibarra, H. (2016). *Why Strategic Networking Is Harder for Women.*

Inkson, K., Gunz, H., Ganesh, S., & Roper, J. (2012). "Boundaryless Careers: Bringing Back Boundaries." *Organization Studies* 33 (3): 323–340.

Jaccard, J. (2001). Interaction Effects in Logistic Regression (vol. 135). New York: Sage Publications.

James, E. H. & Wooten, L. P. (2006). "Diversity Crises: How Firms Manage Discrimination Lawsuits." Academy of Management Journal 49 (6): 1103–1118.

Johnson, S. K., Murphy, S. E., Zewdie, S., & Reichard, R. J. (2008). "The Strong, Sensitive Type: Effects of Gender Stereotypes and Leadership Prototypes on the Evaluation of Male and Female Leaders." *Organizational Behavior and Human Decision Processes* 106 (1): 39–60.

"ICMA Survey Research: 2012 State of the Profession Survey Results." (2013). Washington, D.C: International City-County Management Association. https://icma.org/sites/default/files/305096_ICMA%202012%20State%20of%20the%20Profession%20Survey%20Results.pdf

Joseph, D., Boh, W. F, Ang, S., & Slaughter, S. (2012). "The Career Paths Less (or More) Traveled: A Sequence Analysis of IT Career Histories, Mobility Patterns, and Career Success." *MIS Quarterly* 36 (2): 427–452.

Judge, E. (2003). "Women on Board: Help or Hindrance?" Times, November, 21.

Kaatz, J., French, E., & Prentiss-Cooper, H. (1999). "City Council Conflict as a Cause of Psychological Burnout and Voluntary Turnover among City Managers." *State and Local Government Review* 31 (3): 162–172.

Kahneman, D. & Tyersky, A. (1979). "Prospect Theory: An Analysis of Decision under Risk." *Econometrica* 47 (2): 263–292.

Kammerer, G, Farris, C., DeGrove, J., & Clubok, A. (1962). *City Managers in Politics: An Analysis of Manager Tenure and Termination.* Gainesville, FL: University of Florida Press.

Kanter, R. M. (1977). "Some Effects of Proportions on Group Life: Skewed Sex Ratios and Responses to Token Women." *American Journal of Sociology* 82 (5): 965–990.

Kioko, S., Marlowe, J., Matkin, D. S. T., Moody, M., Smith, D. L., & Zhao, Z. J. (2011). "Why Public Financial Management Matters." *Journal of Public Administration Research and Theory* 21 (suppl_1): i113–i124.

King, A. G. & Spruell, S. P. (2001). "Coca-Cola Takes High Road." *Black Enterprise* 31 (7). https://elibrary.ru/page_404.asp?qx=https%3A%2F%2Felibrary%2Eru%2Fitem%2Easp%3Fid%3D4085540.

Kram, K.E. (1985). *Mentoring at Work: Developmental Relationships in Organizational Life.* Glenview, IL: Scott, Forestman.

Lee, Y. & Tang, F. (2015). "More Caregiving, Less Working: Caregiving Roles and Gender Difference." *Journal of Applied Gerontology* 34 (4): 465–483. https://doi.org/10.1177/0733464813508649.

Levenshtein, V. I. (1966). "Binary Codes Capable of Correcting Deletions, Insertions and Reversals." *Cybernetics and Control Theory* 10 (8): 707–771.

Lowi, T. J. (1985). *The State in Politics: The Relation between Policy and Administration.* Regulatory Policy and the Social Sciences. Berkeley, CA: University of California Press.

MacIndoe, H. & Abbott, A. (2004). *Sequence Analysis and Optimal Matching Techniques for Social Science Data.* Handbook of Data Analysis. London: Sage Publications. https://dx.doi.org/10.4135/9781848608184.n17.

McCabe, B., Feiock, R., Clingermayer, J., & Stream, G. (2008). "Turnover among City Managers: The Role of Political and Economic Change." *Public Administration Review* 62 (2): 380–386.

McGuire, G. M. (2002). Gender, race, and the shadow structure: A study of informal networks and inequality in a work organization. *Gender & Society* 16 (3): 303–322.

McPherson, M., Smith-Lovin, L., & Cook, J. M. (2001). "Birds of a Feather: Homophily in Social Networks." *Annual Review of Sociology* 27 (1): 415–444.

Metz, I. & Tharenou, P. (2001). "Women's Career Advancement: The Relative Contribution of Human and Social Capital." *Group & Organization Management* 26 (3): 312–342.

Miller, W., Kerr, B., & Reid, M. (1999). "A National Study of Gender-Based Occupational Segregation in Municipal Bureaucracies: Persistence of Glass Walls?" *Public Administration Review* 59 (3): 218–230.

Mohr, J. (1976). "Task Force on Women in the Profession." ICMA. https://icma .org/sites/default/files/Women%20in%20the%20Profession%20Task% 20Force%20Final%20Report%20July%201976.pdf

Mooi, E. & Sarstedt, M. (2011). *A Concise Guide to Market Research: The Process, Data, and Methods Using IBM SPSS Statistics*. Heidelberg: Springer.

Nelson, K. & Stenberg, C. (2017). *Managing Local Government: An Essential Guide for Municipal and County Managers*. Chapel Hill, NC. https://us .sagepub.com/en-us/nam/managing-local-government/book246298#contents.

Nelson, K. L. & Stenberg, C. W. (2018). *Managing Local Government: An Essential Guide for Municipal and County Managers*. Thousand Oaks, CA: CQ Press, an imprint of Sage Publications.

Nelson, K. L. & Svara, J. H. (2010). "Adaptation of Models versus Variations in Form: Classifying Structures of City Government." *Urban Affairs Review* 45 (4): 544–562.

Nelson, K. & Nollenberger, K. (2011). "Conflict and Cooperation in Municipalities: Do Variations in Form of Government Have an Effect?" *Urban Affairs Review* 47 (5): 969–720. https://doi.org/10.1177 /1078087411409129.

Padavic, I., Ely, R. J., & Reid, E. M. (2020). "Explaining the Persistence of Gender Inequality: The Work–Family Narrative as a Social Defense against the 24/7 Work Culture." *Administrative Science Quarterly* 65 (1): 61–111.

Pandey, S. & Amezcua, A. S. (2018). "Women's Business Ownership and Women's Entrepreneurship through the Lens of US Federal Policies." *Small Business Economics* 1–30.

Patton, M. (1990). *Qualitative Evaluation and Research Methods*. Beverly Hills, CA: Sage Publications.

Peterson, H. (2016). "Is Managing Academics 'Women's Work'? Exploring the Glass Cliff in Higher Education Management." *Educational Management Administration & Leadership* 44 (1): 112–127.

Phillips, K. W., Dumas T. L., & Rothbard, N. P. (2018). "Diversity and Authenticity." *Harvard Business Review*, no. March–April 2018 (March). https://hbr.org/2018/03/diversity-and-authenticity.

Pierson, P. (2000). "Increasing Returns, Path Dependence, and the Study of Politics." *American Political Science Review* 94 (2): 251–267.

Podolny, J. M. & Baron, J. N. (1997). "Resources and Relationships: Social Networks and Mobility in the Workplace." *American Sociological Review* 62 (5): 673–693.

Portillo, S. & DeHart-Davis, L. (2009). "Gender and Organizational Rule Abidance." *Public Administration Review* 69(2), 339–347.

Rainey, Hal G. (2009). *Understanding and Managing Public Organizations*. San Francisco, CA: Jossey-Bass.

Rawski, S. L. & Workman-Stark, A. L. (2018). "Masculinity Contest Cultures in Policing Organizations and Recommendations for Training Interventions." *Journal of Social Issues* 74 (3): 607–627. https://doi.org/10.1111/josi.12286.

Renner, T. & DeSantis, V. (1994). "City Manager Turnover: The Impact of Formal Authority and Electoral Change." *State & Local Government Review* 23 (2): 104–111.

Riccucci, N. M. (2009). "The Pursuit of Social Equity in the Federal Government: A Road Less Traveled?" *Public Administration Review*, 69 (3): 373–382.

Riccucci, N. (2018). *Managing Diversity in Public Sector Workforces: Essentials of Public Policy and Administration Series*. Boulder, CO: Routledge.

Ridgeway, C. L. (1997). "Interaction and the Conservation of Gender Inequality: Considering Employment." *American Sociological Review*, 218–235.

Ridgeway, C. L. (2001). "Gender, Status, and Leadership." *Journal of Social Issues* 57 (4): 637–655.

Rivenbark, W. C., Roenigk, D. J., & Allison, G. S. (2010). "Conceptualizing Financial Condition in Local Government." *Journal of Public Budgeting, Accounting & Financial Management* 22 (2): 149–177.

Roberts, L. M., Mayo, A. J., Ely, R. J., & Thomas, D. A. (2018). "Beating the Odds." *Harvard Business Review* 96 (2): 126–131.

Romzek, B. S. & Dubnick, M. J. (1987). "Accountability in the Public Sector: Lessons from the Challenger Tragedy." *Public Administration Review* 47 (3): 227–238.

Rosette, A. S., Koval, C. Z., Ma, A., & Livingston, R. (2016). "Race Matters for Women Leaders: Intersectional Effects on Agentic Deficiencies and Penalties." *The Leadership Quarterly* 27 (3): 429–445.

Roth, L. M. (2006). *Selling Women Short: Gender and Money on Wall Street.* Princeton, NJ: Princeton University Press.

Rubin, C. (1973). "Where Are the Women in Management?" *Public Management* (February): 8–9.

Ryan, M. K. & Haslam, S. A. (2005). "The Glass Cliff: Evidence That Women Are Over-Represented in Precarious Leadership Positions." *British Journal of Management* 16 (2): 81–90.

   (2007). "The Glass Cliff: Exploring the Dynamics Surrounding the Appointment of Women to Precarious Leadership Positions." *Academy of Management Review* 32 (2): 549–572. https://doi.org/10.5465/amr.2007.24351856.

Ryan, M. K., Haslam, S. A., Hersby, M. D., & Bongiorno, R. (2011). "Think Crisis–Think Female: The Glass Cliff and Contextual Variation in the Think Manager–Think Male Stereotype." *Journal of Applied Psychology* 96 (3): 470–484.

Ryan, M. K, Haslam, S. A., Moregnroth, T., Rink F., Stoker, J., & Peters, K. (2016). "Getting on Top of the Glass Cliff: Reviewing a Decade of Evidence, Explanations, and Impact." *The Leadership Quarterly* 27: 446–455.

Sabharwal, M. (2013). "From Glass Ceiling to Glass Cliff: Women in Senior Executive Service." *Journal of Public Administration Research and Theory* 25 (2): 399–426. https://doi.org/10.1093/jopart/mut030.

Saidel, J. R. & Loscocco, K. (2005). "Agency Leaders, Gendered Institutions, and Representative Bureaucracy." *Public Administration Review* 65 (2): 158–170.

Sanchez-Hucles, J. V. & Davis, D. D. (2010). "Women and Women of Color in Leadership: Complexity, Identity, and Intersectionality." *American Psychologist* 65 (3): 171.

Santen, B. & Donker, H. (2009). "Board Diversity in the Perspective of Financial Distress: Empirical Evidence from the Netherlands." *Corporate Board: Role, Duties and Composition* 5: 23–35.

Schein, V. E. (1975). "Relationships between Sex Role Stereotypes and Requisite Management Characteristics among Female Managers." *Journal of Applied Psychology* 60 (3): 340–344.

Schepker, D. J. & Barker, V. L. III. (2018). "How Stigmatized Are Dismissed Chief Executives? The Role of Character Questioning Causal Accounts and Executive Capital in Dismissed CEO Reemployment." *Strategic Management Journal* 39 (9): 2566–2586.

Slack, J. D. (1987). "Affirmative Action and City Managers: Attitudes toward Recruitment of Women." *Public Administration Review* (March/April): 199–206.

Slaughter, A. M. (2012). "Why Women Still Can't Have It All." The Atlanatic, August.

Smith, A. E. (2015). "On the Edge of a Glass Cliff: Women in Leadership in Public Organizations." *Public Administration Quarterly* 29 (3): 484 517.

Smith, A. E. & Hatmaker, D. M. (2017). "Individual Stresses and Strains in the Ascent to Leadership: Gender, Work, and Family." In Madsen, S. R. (ed.) *Handbook of Research on Gender and Leadership* (pp. 304–315). Cheltenham: Edward Elgar Publishing.

Smith, A. E, Hatmaker, D. M., & Subedi, S. (2015). *Climbing the Ladder: Gender Differences in the Careers of Federal Agency Leaders.* Vancouver, BC. https://journals.aom.org/doi/abs/10.5465/ambpp .2015.16742abstract.

Smith, A. E. & Monaghan, K. R. (2013). "Some Ceilings Have More Cracks: Representative Bureaucracy in Federal Regulatory Agencies." *American Review of Public Administration* 43 (1): 50–71. https://doi.org/10.1177 /0275074011420997.

Stazyk, E. C. & Frederickson, H. G. (eds.) (2018). *Handbook of American Public Administration.* Cheltenham: Edward Elgar Publishing.

Stivers, C. (2002). *Gender Images in Public Administration: Legitimacy and the Administrative State.* Thousand Oaks, CA: Sage Publications.

Stout, J. G., & Dasgupta, N. (2011). "When He Doesn't Mean You: Gender-Exclusive Language as Ostracism." *Personality and Social Psychology Bulletin* 37 (6): 757–769.

Strauss, A. & Corbin, J. (1998). *Basics of Qualitative Research Techniques.* Thousand Oaks, CA: Sage Publications.

Sun, S. L., Zhu, J., & Ye, K. (2015). "Board Openness during an Economic Crisis." *Journal of Business Ethics* 129 (2): 363–377.

Sutton, R. I. & Callahan, A. J. (1987). "The Stigma of Bankruptcy: Spoiled Organizational Image and Its Management." *Academy of Management Journal* 30 (3): 405–436.

Svara, J. (1990). *Official Leadership in the City: Patterns of Conflict and Cooperation.* New York: Oxford University Press.

Terjesen, S., Aguilera, R. V., & Lorenz, R. (2015). "Legislating a Woman's Seat on the Board: Institutional Factors Driving Gender Quotas for Boards of Directors." *Journal of Business Ethics* 128 (2): 233–251. https://doi.org/10 .1007/s10551-014-2083-1.

Tsui, A. S. & O'reilly III, C. A. (1989). "Beyond Simple Demographic Effects: The Importance of Relational Demography in Superior–Subordinate Dyads." *Academy of Management Journal* 32 (2): 402–423.

US Equal Employment Opportunity Commission. (2018). "Enforcement and Litigation Statistics."

Meindl, J. R., Ehrlich, S. B., & Dukerich, J. M., (1985). "The Romance of Leadership" *Administrative Science Quarterly* 30 (1): 78–102.

Thomas, K. M. & Wise, P. G. (1999). "Organizational Attractiveness and Individual Differences: Are Diverse Applicants Attracted by Different Factors?" *Journal of Business and Psychology* 13 (3): 375–390. https://doi .org/10.1023/A:1022978400698.

Van Maanen, J. V. & Schein, E. H. (1979). "Toward a Theory of Organizational Socialization." *Research in Organizational Behavior* 2: 209–264. https:// dspace.mit.edu/bitstream/handle/1721.1/1934/?sequence=1

Vecchio, R. P. (2002). "Leadership and Gender Advantage." *The Leadership Quarterly* 13: 643–671.

Velte, P. (2018). "Appointing Female CEOS in Risky and Precarious Firm Circumstances: A Review of the Glass Cliff Phenomenon." *Corporate Ownership & Control* 15 (2): 33–43.

Ward Jr., J. H. (1963). "Hierarchical Grouping to Optimize an Objective Function." *Journal of the American Statistical Association* 58 (201): 236–244.

Warner, J., Watts, R., & Wruck, K. (1988). "Stock Prices and Top Management Changes." *Journal of Financial Economics* 20: 461–492.

Watson, D. & Hassett, W. (2003). "Long-Serving City Managers: Why Do They Stay?" *Long-Serving City Managers: Why Do They Stay?* 63 (1): 71–78. https://doi.org/10.1111/1540–6210.00265

Watson, D. J. & Hassett, W. L. (2004). "Career Paths of City Managers in America's Largest Council-Manager Cities." *Public Administration Review* 64 (2): 192–199.

Wentling, R. M. & Palma-Rivas, N. (1997). "Current Status and Future Trends of Diversity Initiatives in the Workplace: Diversity Experts' Perspectives." Berkeley, CA: National Center for Research in Vocational Education. https://files.eric.ed.gov/fulltext/ED414474.pdf.

Wesolowski, M. A. & Mossholder, K. W. (1997). "Relational Demography in Supervisor–Subordinate Dyads: Impact on Subordinate Job Satisfaction, Burnout, and Perceived Procedural Justice." *Journal of Organizational Behavior* 18 (4): 351–362.

Wilkins, V. M. & Williams, B. N. (2009). "Representing Blue: Representative Bureaucracy and Racial Profiling in the Latino Community." *Administration & Society* 40 (8): 775–798.

Williams, C. L. (1992). "The 'Glass Escalator': Hidden Advantages for Men in the 'Female' Professions." *Social Problems* 39 (3): 253–267.

(1995). *Still a Man's World*. Berkeley, CA: University of California Press. www.ucpress.edu/book/9780520087873/still-a-mans-world.

Williams, J. C., Blair-Loy, M., & Berdahl, J. L. (2013). "Cultural Schemas, Social Class, and the Flexibility Stigma." *Journal of Social Issues* 69 (2): 209 234.

Williams, M. J. & Tiedens, L. Z. (2015). "A Meta-Analysis of Penalties for Women's Implicit and Explicit Leadership Behaviors." In *Academy of Management Proceedings* (Vol. 2015, No. 1, p. 17293). Briarcliff Manor, NY: Academy of Management.

Wright, P., Ferris, S., Hiller, J., & Kroll, M. (1995). "Competitiveness through Management of Diversity: Effects on Stock Price Valuation." *The Academy of Management Journal* 38 (1): 272–287. https://doi.org/10.2307/256736.

Yoder, J. D. (1991). "Rethinking Tokenism: Looking beyond Numbers." *Gender & Society* 5 (2): 178–192.

Public and Nonprofit Administration

Andrew Whitford

University of Georgia

Andrew Whitford is Alexander M. Crenshaw Professor of Public Policy in the School
of Public and International Affairs at the University of Georgia. His research
centers on strategy and innovation in public policy and organization studies.

Robert Christensen

Brigham Young University

Robert Christensen is professor and George Romney Research Fellow
in the Marriott School at Brigham Young University. His research focuses on
prosocial and antisocial behaviors and attitudes in public and nonprofit organizations.

About the Series

The foundations of this series are cutting-edge contributions on emerging topics and
definitive reviews of keystone topics in public and nonprofit administration, especially
those that lack longer treatment in textbook or other formats. Among keystone topics of
interest for scholars and practitioners of public and nonprofit administration, it covers
public management, public budgeting and finance, nonprofit studies, and the interstitial
space between the public and nonprofit sectors, along with theoretical and methodo-
logical contributions, including quantitative, qualitative, and mixed-methods pieces.

The Public Management Research Association

The Public Management Research Association improves public governance
by advancing research on public organizations, strengthening links among
interdisciplinary scholars, and furthering professional and academic
opportunities in public management.

Cambridge Elements ≡

Public and Nonprofit Administration

Elements in the Series

Motivating Public Employees
Marc Esteve and Christian Schuster

*Organizational Obliviousness: Entrenched Resistance to Gender Integration
in the Military*
Alesha Doan and Shannon Portillo

Partnerships that Last: Identifying the Keys to Resilient Collaboration
Heather Getha-Taylor

*Behavioral Public Performance: How People Make Sense
of Government Metrics*
Oliver James, Donald P. Moynihan, Asmus Leth Olsen and
Gregg G. Van Ryzin

Redefining Development: Resolving Complex Challenges in Developing Countries
Jessica Kritz

Gender Imbalance in Public Sector Leadership
Leisha DeHart-Davis, Deneen Hatmaker, Kimberly L. Nelson, Sanjay K. Pandey,
Sheela Pandey and Amy E. Smith

A full series listing is available at: www.cambridge.org/EPNP

Printed in the United States
By Bookmasters